Web 2.0 Applications in Library

Web 2.0 Applications in Library

Shankar Ashok Dhande
Librarian
J.E.S., Vaidyanath College
(Arts Commerce and Science)
Parli Vaidyanath Dist Beed. (M.S.) 431515

Ess Ess Publications
New Delhi

Web 2.0 Applications in Library

ISBN: 978-81-7000-720-3

₹ 500/-

First Published 2014

Published by:
Ess Ess Publications
4831/24, Ansari Road,
Darya Ganj,
New Delhi-110 002.
INDIA
Phones: 23260807, 41563444
Fax: 41563334
E-mail: info@essessreference.com
www.essessreference.com

Cover Design by *Patch Creative Unit*

Printed and bound in India at Salasar Imaging Systems.

Contents

Preface

In this era use of virtual communication is increasing in every way of life. Users are applying new ways to find information useful to them. Use of social networking portals for information communication is on the rise. Constant flow of information through all the sources makes one get the feeling of 'Information Explosion', therefore the library professionals also need to connect the user whichever way it is comfortable for the user to receive information. Though the entire world is connected very comprehensively through social networking portals, we try to dig deeper and explain how the optimum dissemination of information can be done and what role does the latest cutting edge technology plays in our day-to-day life. Readers would find that this book talks about almost everything there is to know about latest modes of communication. The chapter-wise break-up is presented below to show as to how this book systematically covers all the aspects related to everything there is to know about cutting edge technology.

First Chapter, **Library and Web Technology** explains Web 2.0 definitions, terminological changes shift from Web 1.0 to Web 2.0., Characteristics of Web 2.0, Web Technology Availability and Use in the Social Networking Software, Meaning of Library 2.0 and its Definitional Analysis and Principle of Library 2.0 and its Practice in the Library, and The Challenges of Library 2.0 in Indian Libraries.

Second Chapter, **Web 2.0 Tools and Their Application in the Library** explains the types of social tools of web 2.0, social networking sites and benefits of social networking explaining in detail all such tools such as Blogs, Free Web for Information Collection and Dissemination, Blog Definitional Analysis, Tips for Bloggers, Characteristics of blog, Function as Marketing of Library Services, Blog use in Library, Use of Facebook in Library, Facebook applications for Libraries, Facebook User's Guidelines, Library Services on Twitter, Its Impact on Library Services, Reference Services and Current Awareness Services, Wikis and its Characteristics such as browsing editing and resource review collections, event planning and other uses of Wikis, Podcasting and Vodcasting and their use in Library, Social Bookmarking: Its Definition, Advantages and Disadvantages, Social Bookmarking and Educational Benefits of Social Bookmarking, Social Bookmarking Tips, Evaluation Features, How to Post Bookmarks, Social Bookmarking Tools, DELICIOUS DIIGO use in the Library, Tagging, Instant Messaging, Instant Messaging Technologies, Characteristics of Instant Messaging, Steps for Setting up Instant Messaging Services, Selection of Instant Messaging System and Software, Online Videos, YouTube Functions and Use, Reach Site Summary, Introduction RSS Feed, Reader RSS History, RSS Use in Library Services, Steps Involved in Using RSS Feeds, How to Get RSS Feed Reader, How to Get Content for Selected Feeds, FLICKR and its Use in Library for Pictorial Views and MASHUPS and its Functions in a Library.

Chapter Third **Changing Skill and Competency of a Librarian** describes Library 2.0, Application of Web 2.0 Tools in Library, Objectives of the Library 2.0 in the Present Situation, Required Skill and Competencies for a Library Professionals in ICT Era. This chapter also goes on to discuss in detail, many latest and must-know terms such as Information, Computer, Communication, Multimedia, CD

ROM, Networking, Barcoding, Digital and Virtual Technology, etc. This chapter further discusses Higher Educational Policy Initiatives and The Role of National Knowledge Commission of India. Finally there is coverage of Knowledge Management with Library 2.0 Tools use in library services.

It is hoped that with the comprehensive coverage given to topics covered, this book shall be a welcome addition to the bookshelves of the students, librarians, teachers and decision makers at all levels.

Acknowledgements

I would like to record my appreciation for Vaidyanath College Principal Dr. R.K. Ippar and Senior Professor Dr. D.V. Meshram for always encouraging me to write this book. I also thank the library staff of my institution for their valuable cooperation extended to me in preparation of the book in hand. I specially thank my parents who have always given me opportunities to learn and teach and last but not the least, I thank my wife for her constant support and encouragement.

1

Library and Web Technology

"We have to meet our users where they are with tools they can [use] and are comfortable using." —**Anonymous**

Web 2.0 : World Wide Web or web 1.0 is greatest success in the history. The term web 2.0 was firstly conceptualized and made popular by Tim O' Reilly and Dale Dougherty O'Reilly Media in 2004. They describe the trends and business models which survived the technology sector market crash of the 1990s. Web 2.0 suggests a new version of the World Wide Web. It does not refer to an update to any technical specification, but rather to increasing changes in the ways software developers and users use the Web. A Web 2.0 site may allow users to interact and collaborate with each other in society. As a content generator in virtual community, user can freely communicate by web 2.0. In 1.0 version people had limited content access. Web 2.0 includes tools like social networking sites, as Blogs, wikis, Youtubes mushup folksonomies. World Wide Web Inventor Tim Berners Lee Described the term as Jargon It is very different than prior web technology. His original vision of the Web was "a collaborative medium, a place where we could all **meet**, read and write".

Web 2.0 Definitions : As above we have seen introductory part of web 2.0. Now it is essential to define web 2.0 as.

Dictionary Definition : "A second generation in the development of the world wide web, conceived as a combination of concept, trends, and technologies that focus on user collaboration, sharing of user generated content, and social networking. The internet viewed as a medium in which interactive experience, in the form of blogs, wikis, forums, etc plays a more important role than simply accessing information.

Also defined by Tim O'Reilly in (2004) "Web 2.0 is the business revolution in the computer industry caused by the move to the Internet as platform and an attempt to understand the rules for success on that new platform."

Wikipedia described that, "Web 2.0 is a trend in World Wide Web technology and web design, a second generation of web-based communities and hosted services such as social-networking sites, wikis, blogs, and folksonomies, which aim to facilitate creativity, collaboration, and sharing among users."

Macaskill and Owen (2006) have defined Web 2.0 tools as a "web-based platform which allows users to gain access, contribute, describe, harvest, tag, annotate and bookmark Web mediated content in various formats, such as text, video, audio, pictures and graphs.

Also, Stuart (2010) has defined Web 2.0 tools as sites which share stuff. Some of the Web 2.0 based popular websites are Flickr which can be used to share Photos, YouTube for sharing videos, Last for sharing audio, and MySpace for sharing text based information. The web 2.0 is

Read/Write Web and Social and Information consumers, contributors are often one in the same.

The concept of web as participatory platform captures many of these characteristics. Bart Decrem, a founder and former CEO of Flock, calls Web 2.0 the "participatory Web" and regards the Web-as-information-source as Web 1.0.

CHANGES INTO WEB 1.0 TO 2.0 : Web 1.0 to 2.0 phenomenon changes are given as following, like Web 2.0 is second generation collaborative, participative web.

WEB 1.0	WEB 2.0
Reading	Writing
Companies	Communities
Personals Websites	Blogs
Owning	Sharing
Taxonomy	Tags
Britannica Online	Wikipedia
Domain Name Speculation	Search Engine Optimization
Page Views	Cost per Click
Screen Scraping	Web Services
Publishing	Participation
Content Management System	Wikis
Directories (taxonomy)	Tagging (Folksonomy)
Stickiness	Syndication

Web 2.0 websites allow users to do more than just retrieve information. Web 2.0 offers the user with more user-interface, software and storage facilities. All is possible by their browser. This has been called "network as platform" for computing. Major features of Web 2.0 include social networking sites, user created web sites, self-publishing platforms, tagging, and social bookmarking. Users can provide the data that is on a Web 2.0 site and exercise some control over that data. These sites may have an "architecture of participation" that encourages users to add value to the application as they use it. Some scholars have made the case

that Cloud Computing is a form of Web 2.0 because cloud computing is simply an implication of computing on the Internet.

Web 2.0 offers all users the same freedom to contribute. While this opens the possibility for serious debate and teamwork. According to Best, the characteristics of Web 2.0 are: rich user experience, user participation, dynamic content, Metadata, web standards and scalability further characteristics, such as openness, freedom and collaborative work intelligence by way of user participation, can also be viewed as essential attributes of Web 2.0. Web 2.0 is not a software package, nor even a collection of programs.

Characteristic of Web 2.0 : web 2.0 has essential characteristics to identify its usefulness in information society; web 2.0 has characteristics as following.

1. **Openness :** As above definitional analysis web 2.0 is open to all no hesitance to any user all over the world and discipline. Web 2.0 is open for all types of people, to share ideas and views on various topics.
2. **Networked Data :** Web 2.0 is combination of network that interactive in nature and in the network data is accessible.
3. **Participative :** Web 2.0 is varying participative in nature each and every tools of web 2.0 require participation from the end user. It allow user to share and participate as blogging sharing files of uploading snaps.
4. **Sharing in Nature :** Tools is share ideas with all created groups and can share views that is benefits to create library online community.
5. **Change :** As human nature change the web 2.0 face could be change because it is depends upon human nature of work types of ideas and views.

6. **Informative Within groups :** Web 2.0 tools informative in nature every sort of information we can put and share within our community. Therefore the community can reply immediately on the shared information.
7. **Communicative within group :** Web 2.0 is also communicative because we can communicate ideas, signs, and symbols in to the created groups. Also it is updating each and every time and expanding its characteristic around the world and hence it is very popular within the library and information science community and library user to apply in the library services and management of library services. To connect library users by the most popular web 2.0 librarian need to reach by this means of tools and techniques developed in modern web technology.

Following figure of web 2.0 Characteristics is showing the scope of web 2.0 in society how web 2.0 is applied in the society, in audio, video, multimedia, text and pictorial format is available in every format which user interest is as blog, wikis, RSS, and Social Network Software's. Standardization, usability, convergence, remix ability, economy and participation are the most important characteristics of the web 2.0

Web 2.0 Characteristics shown in the following Fig. 1.

WEB 2.0 MEME MAP

This "meme map "is intended to summaries the key aspects of Web2.0 in a visual way, using color and text size to indicate importance of web 2.0 . The figure was developed at a brainstorming session during FOO camp a conference at O 'Reilly Media.

Web 2.0 Web features and techniques:

- **Search :** Weblog search, friends search on face book, search presentations on various topics, search snaps on flickr and all search features.

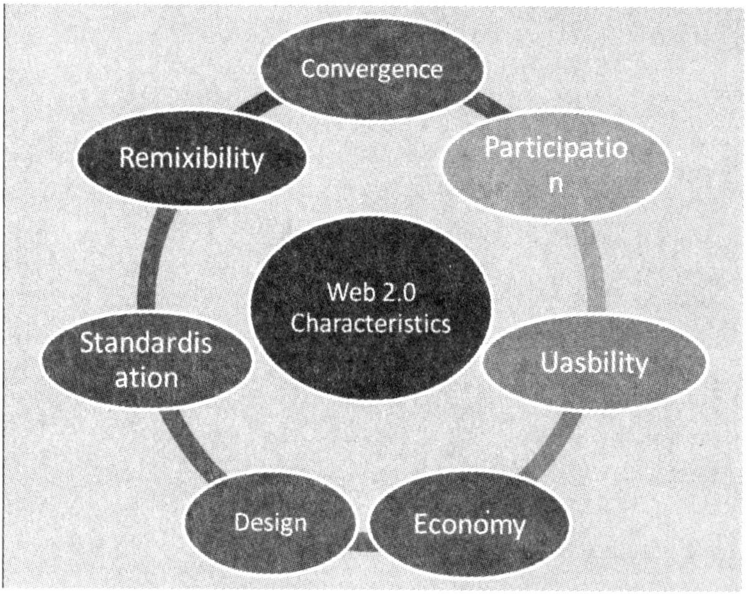

Fig. 1. Web 2.0 Characteristics

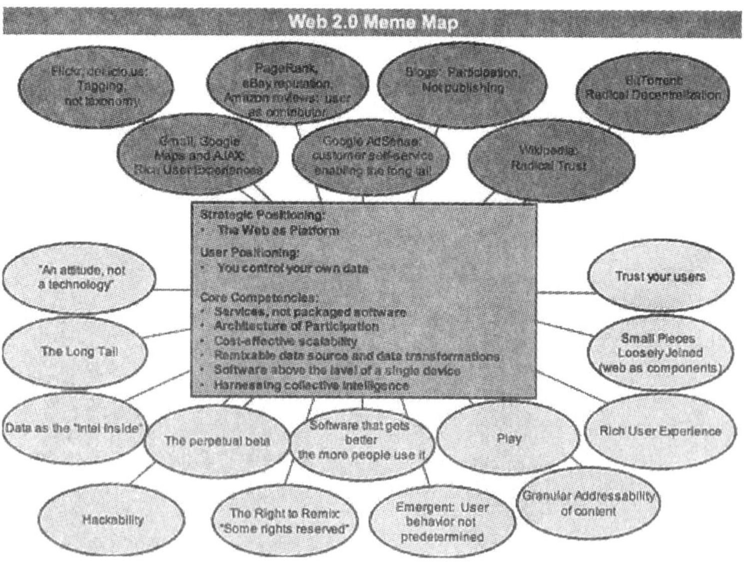

Fig. 2. Web 2.0 Meme Map

http://www.oreillynet.com/pub/a/oreilly/tim/news/
2005/09/30/what-is-web-20.html

- **Links :** Links is another features, web 2.0 all links as web pages of periodicals online book links, blog links is possible through web 2.0
- **Authoring :** Multiple authors can create content in web 2.0 tools as for example wikis.
- **Tags :** Tagging is another feature in web 2.0 tools it tools for tagging informative documents in related keywords.
- **Aggregation :** Web 2.o collection or aggregation of syndication or web content information example is R.S.S.
- **AJAX (asynchronous JavaScript and XML) :** Web 2.0 tools are based on AJAX technologies as Java and XML for creation of the web technologies AJAX is important.
- **API (application Programming interface) :** Web 2.0 has application Programming Interface so it is very easy to use and get required information.
- **Virtual Architecture :** It has virtual architecture for display information it is totally online function for web user.

IMPORTANCE OF WEB 2.0 TOOLS

The Web 2.0 tools have a pervasive impact on society. They allow users to create, describe, post, search, collaborate, share and communicate online content in various forms, ranging from music and bookmarks to photographs and documents. Users can create content via Web 2.0 tools; social networking using mobile phones, etc. will have a significant impact on higher education.

IMPORTANCE OF WEB 2.0

1.Collaborative Content Creation : Web 2.0 tools can create content for that it is important in research and development. It facilitate collaborative content creation.

2. Social Communication : It is social reach in information tools for society. To communicate within our society it is essential for social communication.

3. Express Ideas : Web 2.0 tools are useful for expression of ideas and thoughts, on line.

4. Politically sensible : These tools are important because of that connected with society as well as groups. So these tools are be politically sensible and hence tools have importance.

5. Impact on Higher Education : Basic impact on Higher education is on Teaching and learning tools on higher education. Impact on Library and information services and library community library this enhance the importance of web 2.0 tools.

Web 2.0 Concern : Following types of concerns are while using the web 2.0 tools. So, as we have seen various types of benefits and facilities to our user community but some of the concerns are as following.

- Services
- Security
- Stability
- Privacy
- Time
- Resources
- Staff
- Relevance

As shown in following figure web 2.0 has some basic concerns, although it has much more importance in society. The following figures are much more visual to see the concerns of web 2.0.

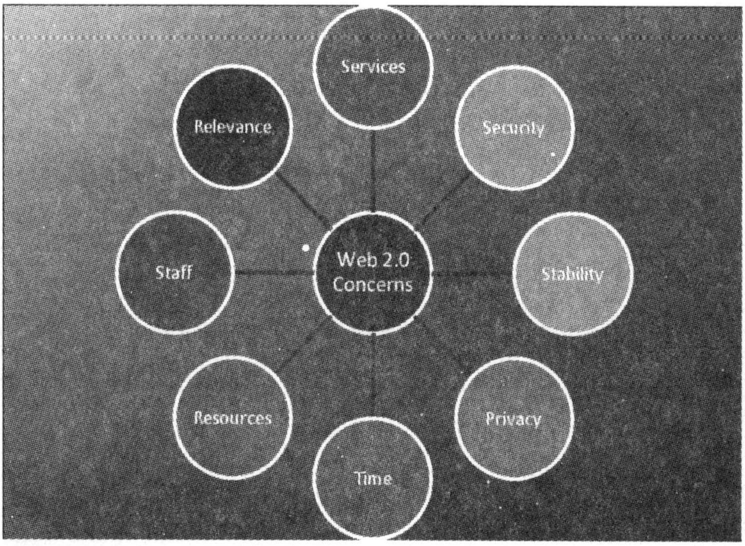

Fig. 2. Web 2.0 Concerns

WEB TECHNOLOGY

Ajax and JavaScript frameworks : Web browser technologies used in Web 2.0 development include Ajax and JavaScript frameworks. Ajax programming uses JavaScript to upload and download new data from the web server without undergoing a full page reload. To allow users to continue to interact with the page, communications such as data requests going to the server are separated from data coming back to the page. The data fetched by an Ajax request is typically formatted in XML or JSON (JavaScript Object Notation) format; two widely used structured data formats. Since both of these formats are natively understood by JavaScript, a programmer can easily use them to transmit structured data in their web application. When this data is received via Ajax, the JavaScript program then uses the Document object model (DOM) to dynamically update the web page based on the new data, allowing for a rapid and interactive user experience. In short, using these techniques, Web designers can make their pages function like desktop applications. For example, Google Docs uses this technique to create a Web based word processor.

ADOBE FLEX : It is another technology often used in Web 2.0 applications. Compared to JavaScript, Flex makes it easier for programmers to populate large data grids, charts, and other heavy user interactions. Applications programmed in Flex are compiled and displayed as Adobe Flash Player within the browser. As a widely available plugin independent of W3C standards (the World Wide Web Consortium is the governing body of web standards and protocols), Flash is capable of doing many things that were not possible pre-HTML-5, the language used to construct web pages. Of Flash's various capabilities, the mainly used in Web 2.0 is its ability to play audio and video files. This has allowed for the creation of Web 2.0 sites where video media is seamlessly included with standard HTML. With the introduction of HTML5 in 2010, the role of Flash is decreasing. HTML5 video has been proven to decrease the amount of computer resources required.

Ajax frameworks : In addition to Flash and Ajax, JavaScript/Ajax frameworks have recently become a very popular means of creating Web 2.0 sites. Frameworks smooth over inconsistencies between web browsers and extend the functionality available to developers. On the server side, Web 2.0 uses many of the same technologies as Web 1.0. Languages such as PHP, Ruby, Perl, Python, as well as JSP, and ASP.NET, are used by developers to output data dynamically using information from files and databases. What has begun to change in Web 2.0 is the way this data is formatted. To share its data with other sites, a website must be able to generate output in machine-readable formats such as XML Atom and RSS.

Web 2.0 technologies provide teachers with new ways

to engage students, and even allow student participation on a global level. However, children raised exclusively in the era of new media technologies are less patient with activities such as completion of worksheets and classroom lectures. Decreased participation in a traditional classroom may be due to better feedback received online. By allowing students to use the technology tools of Web 2.0, teachers are giving students the opportunity to share what they learn with peers.

Semantic Web : "Semantic Web" is sometimes used as a synonym for "Web 3.0", though each term's definition varies. "Web where the semantic contents of Web resources are made understandable, not only by humans but also by programs, for a better cooperation among humans and machines" (Berners-Lee). The original 2001 Scientific American article by Berners-Lee described an expected evolution of the existing Web to a Semantic Web, but this has yet to happen. He defines the Semantic Web as "a web of data that can be processed directly and indirectly by machines. The Semantic Web is a collaborative movement led by the international standards body, the World Wide Web (W3C). The standard promotes common data formats on the World. By encouraging the inclusion of semantic content in web pages, the Semantic Web aims at converting the current web dominated by unstructured and semi-structured documents into a "web of data". The Semantic Web stack builds on the W3C's Resource Description Framework (RDF).

According to the W3C, "The Semantic Web provides a common framework that allows data to be shared and reused across application, enterprise, and community boundaries." While its critics have questioned its feasibility, proponents argue that applications in industry, biology and human sciences research have already proven the validity of the original concept. Scholars have explored the social potential of the semantic web in the business and health sectors, and for social networking.

OBJECTIVES

The main purpose of the Semantic Web is driving the

i. **Evolution of the current Web :** by enabling users to find, share, and combine information more easily. Humans are capable of using the Web to carry out tasks such as finding the Estonian translation for "twelve months", reserving a library book, and searching for the lowest price for a DVD.

ii. Machines cannot accomplish all of these tasks without human direction, because web pages are designed to be read by people, not machines. The semantic web is a vision of information that can be readily interpreted by machines, so machines can perform more of the tedious work involved in finding, combining, and acting upon information on the web.

iii. The Semantic Web, as originally envisioned, is a system that enables machines to "understand" and respond to complex human requests based on their meaning. Such an "understanding" requires that the relevant information sources be semantically structured.

Semantic Web : The Semantic Web takes the solution further. It involves publishing in languages specifically designed for data: Resource Description Framework (RDF), Web Ontology Language (OWL), and Extensible Markup Language (XML). HTML describes documents and the links between them. RDF, OWL, and XML, by contrast, can describe arbitrary things such as people, meetings, or airplane parts.

These technologies are combined in order to provide descriptions that supplement or replace the content of Web documents. Thus, content may manifest itself as descriptive data stored in Web-accessible database, or as markup within documents (particularly, in Extensible IITML (XIITML) interspersed with XML, or, more often, purely in XML, with layout or rendering cues stored separately). The machine-readable descriptions enable content managers to add meaning to the content, i.e., to describe the structure of the knowledge we have about that content. In this way, a machine can process knowledge itself, instead of text, using processes similar to human deductive reasoning and inference.

LIBRARY 2.0

The Term Web 2.0 is called second generation of Internet. The term Web 2.0 is describes as an alternative media or medium of communication among Internet users. The idea of Library 2.0 is recent origin, which was derived from the term Web 2.0. The term Library 2.0 was coined by Michael Casey, technology director of a public library in Atlanta, Georgia, USA. Michael Casey first used the term on his blog 'Library crunch' to describe a participatory way of doing librarianship with one's library patrons. Libraries are also using this emerging technology to enhance its present service and generating new services to reach every corner of society which is lagged behind. Web 2.0 offers libraries a platform from where they can interact with their patrons. Appling Web 2.0 technologies on library websites, libraries can encourage participation, collaboration and seek feedback from the user's community. Curran et al. (2007) state that the Web 2.0 offers a means by which data and services previously looked into individual website for reading can be liberated and the reused. It can overcome the barriers between librarians and patrons. Web 2.0 does not replace the existing technology used by libraries but rather adding more value to the services that is provided by the library

Library 2.0 Definition : The term library 2.0 defined by various authors but basic definition by Michael Casey published in Library Journal is, "The heart of Library 2.0 is user- centred change. It is a model for library service that encourages constant and purposeful change, inviting user participation in the creation of both the physical and the virtual services they want, supported by consistently evaluating services. It also attempts to reach new users and better serve current ones through improved customer-driven offerings."

Sarah Houghton, Librarian in Black has defined as "Library 2.0 simply means making your library's space (virtual and physical) more interactive, collaborative, and driven by community needs. Examples of where to start include blogs, gaming nights for teens, and collaborative photo sites. The basic drive is to get people back into the library by making the library relevant to what they want and need in their daily lives to make the library a destination and not an afterthought."

Principles of Library 2.0 : As web 2.0 has principles like that Library 2.0 has following Principles, Library 2.0 has some basic principle about its way of work in communicative society. Therefore library 2.0 has following principles stated by Michael Stephens.

- **The library is everywhere :** Library has no boundary to limit the information access, collect and distribute. Library 2.0 can access everywhere in world and access required information and knowledge. Even Mobile phone can be use as medium for the Library 2.0. So library is everywhere is principle of Library 2.0.
- **The library has no barriers :** Web 2.0 Library has not the barriers. It is direct two way interactions between user and Library 2.0, in user understandable media. This library has no barriers like traffic, mishandling, and insects to destroy the information.

- **The library invites participation :** Library 2.0 is based on participative media sharing library. So it invites user participation and user share knowledge and information. Library 2.0 collects user's participation and views and then displays its views about content on web.
- **The library reaches out to users :** Library 2.0 reaches out to user as well as its similar community. Also Library is not limited to group its content can access beyond boundaries.
- The library is human and recognizes that its users are human.

Library 2.0 in Practice : Library 2.0 is application of web 2.0 for library functions. In practice, Library 2.0 uses these tools to apply in the library functions.

A few generalized examples:

- **Blogs written by library staff :** In practice Library 2.0 is creation of Blogs written by library staff. Update regularly content of the Blog and respond to the library users by Feedback on blog.
- **Flickr accounts showcasing events, etc. :** To Create Account on Flickr and upload photo and display library events.
- **Presence on social networking sites :** Library 2.0 should be presence n the social networking sites for user interaction and solve the difficulties while accessing information.
- **RSS feeds and Comments :** Give Access to the RSS feed and comments to user. RSS feeds can update periodically.
- **Podcasts and Screen casts :** Access podcast and or screen cast and collect for user's point of views.
- **Wikis for reader's advisory and subject guides:**

Design and development of wikis or library portal on wikis to provide the user accessible services.

Library 2.0 Buzz Words for

Connections : As like web 2.0 libraries 2.0 is not possible without connections. Connections can be linking to user's connection to internet and user's connection to information and knowledge.

Communication : Communication of information server and receiver Library 2.0 is rich in various ways. It is effective way to information exchange and transfer in to society.

Collaboration : Library 2.0 enhances collaboration among users. It is collaborative way of content creation. So it way to collaborate thoughts among subject experts, participative way for teaching and learning.

Cooperation : Every user should be participate or co-operate for the content development or information exchange process.

Change : Change is basic factor or signal for human development process. Web 2.0 tools need to change for every time as information update.

Contribution : Library 2.0 is buzz word for contribution of social network users. Contribution in social networking sites is base of success in web 2.0 tools.

Community : The library 2.0 is community building of online social networking tools. It connects society on one platform like twitter face book blog, RSS. So it is Buzz word for above all.

A theory for Library 2.0 could be understood to have these four essential elements:

It is user-centered : Users participate in the creation of the content and services they view within the library's web-presence, OPAC, etc. The consumption and creation of content is dynamic, and thus the roles of librarian and user are not always clear.

It provides a multi-media experience : Both the collections and services of Library 2.0 contain video and audio components. While this is not often cited as a function of Library 2.0, it is here suggested that it should be.

It is socially rich : The library's web-presence includes users' presences. There are both synchronous (e.g. IM) and asynchronous (e.g. wikis) ways for users to communicate with one another and with librarians.

It is communally innovative : This is perhaps the single most important aspect of Library 2.0. It rests on the foundation of libraries as a community service, but understands that as communities change, libraries must not only change with them, and they must allow users to change the library. It seeks to continually change its services, to find new ways to allow communities, not just individuals to seek, find, and utilize information.

The Challenges of Library 2.0 in Indian Library:

1. Financial Crunch
2. Lack of ICT infrastructure
3. Technical Illiteracy in library personnel's and users.
4. Lack of training and orientation program.

Library 2.0 is a user-centered virtual community. It is a socially rich, often autonomous electronic space. While Librarian 2.0 might act as a facilitator and provide support, he or she is not inevitably primarily responsible for the design of the content. Users interact with and create resources with one another and with librarians. In some ways, it is a virtual reality for libraries, a Web manifestation of the library as place. A library's presence on the Web in Library 2.0 includes the existence of that library's community and utilizes the same applications and technologies as its community, a concept recognizes in a very useful model for Library 2.0 in regards to academic libraries.

2

Web 2.0 Tools and Application in Library

A Manager is responsible for the application and performance of knowledge. — **Peter Drucker**

The term Web 2.0 is a boom of the present time. The development of Web 2.0 presents immense opportunity to library professional for interaction and collaborative research. There are number of web based services and application that demonstrate the foundation of web 2.0 concept and they are already being used to a certain extent in library. These technologies are configured for user services and its base is internet which includes. Reilly simple Syndication (RSS), wikis, Weblogs, Photo sharing Flickr, Picasa, Social Networking software, AJAX, and API Programming (Google Map), Streaming media and audio and video formats, personalized alerts, Podcasting and MP3 files, folksonomics, tagging, Social book marking (such as delicious) open source software, user driven rating and open access content.

The social tools of web 2.0 : Social gathering tools of web 2.0 as shown in following figure. Figure display the number of social networking tools which are the mostly useful to provide library services.

Need of Social Software tools : social software need use by following statistical information on internet users. Following types of percent users are engaging the social software or tools. Exploding Growth in information and communication technology and explosion of information create need of social software.

a. MySpace has over 200 million users
b. Facebook has over 53 million users half of which sign in daily
c. Over 75 million blogs
d. Wikipedia has over 5 million articles written in over 200 languages
e. People view over 100 million videos daily on YouTube
f. Flicrk has over 2 billion photos
g. Mainstream Adoption
h. 85% of college students have a Facebook account
i. Americans spend an average of 14 hours per week on the Web
j. 85% of young broadband users have watched online video
k. 51% of American teens have uploaded photos to the Web
l. 55% of American teens have a social networking profile
m. Over half of all visitors to MySpace and over 40% to Facebook are over 35 years old

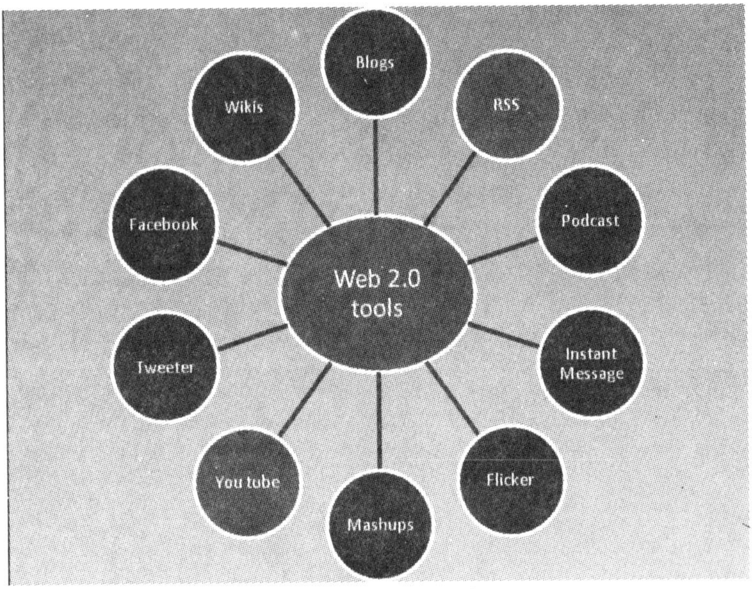

Fig. 4. Web 2.0 tools

SOCIAL NETWORKING

Social networks are perhaps the most promising and embracing technology discussed here. They enable messaging, blogging, streaming media, and tagging, discussed later. MySpace, Face book, Del.icio.us and Flickr are networks that have enjoyed massive popularity in Web 2.0. While MySpace and FaceBook enable users to share themselves with one another detailed profiles of users' lives and personalities, Del.icio.us enables users to share Web resources and Flickr enables the sharing of pictures. Other social networks are noteworthy as well. Library Thing enables users to catalog their books and view what other users share those books. The implications of this site on how librarians recommend reading to users are apparent. Library Thing enables users, thousands of them potentially, to recommend books to one another simply by viewing one another's collections. It also enables them to communicate asynchronously, blog, and "tag" their books. It does not require much imagination to begin seeing a library as a social network itself. In fact, much of libraries' role throughout history has been as a communal gathering place, one of shared identity, communication, and action. Social networking could enable librarians and patrons not only to interact, but to share and change resources dynamically in an electronic medium. Users can create accounts with the library network, see what other users have in common to their information needs, recommend resources to one another, and the network recommends resources to users, based on similar profiles, demographics, previously-accessed sources, and a host of data that users provide. And, of course, these networks would enable users to choose what is public and what is not, a notion that could help circumvent the privacy issues. Following figure showing social networking tools are connected to each other in one web network. So far as social networking sites are connected to its similar software like twitter, facebook, Linked in etc.

Fig. 5. Social Networking tools http://www .brandwatch.com/2011/09/ 10-of-the-weirdest-social-networks/

Types of users applications

New way of communicating : Social networking is

new way of Communicating to the society, It is fast and can be live communication by these social tools of communications like face books chatting instant messaging and other use.

Professional connections : Professional of the same profession come together and forms a group to communicate each other. Therefore library professional use these social tools to communicate each other issues and problems. And also can forms user group or library society.

Applications : Social networking tools application to join the society by the way of web 2.0 and share information and knowledge to society. Therefore Library Professionals use these applications to share library views.

Library profiles : Library profiles can be shown on the social networking sites to know the users about library richness and property of knowledge. Tools like Blog, Wikis, Facebook, Flickr, these tools can show the library profile.

Library services : Application of the social networking to provide library services to community is the basic objectives of the any library professional so by social networking it is easy to communicate society and can provide some basic services like, Current awareness services, Selective Dissemination of Information, Reference service. Like this application are the basic and useful to library community. Also social networking sites can apply on following functions as.

Image sharing : To share images on network and share views on those images.

Photo hosting : To collect the photos on net, to share these photos in library community and store online on web to get anywhere in the world.

Free or low cost : These services can be available by very low cost or can get it on free of cost so to get these services for the student these are network based services can be free of cost for client.

Tagging : Tagging is important in these area of the networking. Tagging use in collaborative work and it is important way to get more and more references to user by social networking sites.

Market library services : Social networking sites are new way to market library services by online by using networking. It can be textual, audio, video, or multimedia, so therefore it is easy to market library services.

- Provide links and information
- Sharing – pictures/music/ideas
- Participation - create a dialog

Get feedback : Every social networking tool has facility to get feedback by networking or social sites. Feed back is measurement of performance the information use.

Table No 1.1 Top ten social networking sites

Rank	Website	URL	Country	Starting Year
1.	Facebook	www.facebook.com	USA	2004
2	Twitter	www.twitter.com	USA	2006
3.	Linkedin	www.linkedin.com	USA	2003
4.	My Space	www.myspace.com	USA	2003
5.	Digg	www.digg.com	USA	2004
6.	Orkut	www.orkut.com	USA	2004
7.	Hi5	www.hi5.com	USA	2003
8	Badoo	www.badoo.com	London	2006
9	Stumbleupon	www.stumbleupon.com	Canada	2001
10	Netlog	www.netlog.com	Belgium	2003

Benefits of social Networking With Reference to Library

Social networking is a recent invention and communication with others is one of the main goals of social networking. People meets online one to another. It offers numerous benefits that could help to grow, personally as well as professionally. The main advantages of social networking include taking to others, building relationship and finding people who are similar to us. The benefits of social networking are as follows.

1. Keeping in touch with user : Library professionals could use these tools for to keep in touch with users as well as our fellow professional.

2. Meet new people : This is very good destination to meet virtual to new people. So to connect to new user this is best to create new fellow or meet people.

3. Get feedback : We professionals can get feedback of web 2.0. Types of user behavior, measure level of satisfaction,

4. Share multiple points of views : It share multiple points of views from the minds of users. Question of multiple views and search information on the views.

5. Linking useful resources : Resources like Book, Periodicals and Others documents can like on those web sites so it benefited to users.

6. Share Information : It can share information and knowledge to users. So it is benefited to exchange information or share information virtually.

7. Communicate freely : Social networking sites are communicative in nature. So it is important to free communication on social networking sites.

8. Create community or group : Library professional can create our users group to provide user services. Group for class, faculty in university, or with special needs is possible with social networking sites.

9. Promotion : To promote library activities best services and library creativity. It is so good for library promotional activity.

10. Job Seeking : Social Networking Sites are so

benefited for Job seeker. Because one can connect to direct recruitment links by these sites and through this job seekers ahs opportunities to Job updates from various sectors, like private and government jobs.

11. Search : Search peoples users or researchers online, search important views of people. Search knowledge from the connected people.

12. Low costs : Use of Social networking sites is very price consuming or low cost services can provide to users as compare to manual services.

BLOG: FREE WEB FOR INFORMATION COLLECTION

Fig. 6. Blog Logo

It is online diaries maintained by an individual. It contains regular entries of commentary, description of event or other materials such as pictures, videos. Blogs are arranged in reverse chronological order. In blogs, old entries are arranged in archives. Libraries are using blogs to bring their users behind the scene to meet staff, introduce with past and present activities and put them in front of row of events. In libraries setting blogs have great application such as current awareness about general news, book reviews and subjects of interest, internal communication, promoting library services and most importantly it encourage user's feedback.

Library blog's can be very effective tools for reaching online. A blog term web log is a discussion or informational site published on the World Wide Web and consisting of discrete entries "posts" typically displayed in reverse chronological order (the most recent post appears first). Until 2009 blogs were usually the work of a single individual, occasionally of a small group, and often covered a single subject. More recently "multi-author blogs" have developed, with posts written by large numbers of authors and professionally edited. Multi Author Blogs from newspapers, other media outlets, universities, interest groups and similar institutions account for an increasing quantity of blog traffic. The rise of Twitter and other "microblogging" systems helps integrate Multi Author Blogs and single-author blogs into societal new streams. Blog can also be used as a verb, meaning to maintain or add content to a blog. As of 16 February 2011, there were over 156 million public blogs in existence. On October 13, 2012, there were around 77 million Tumblr and 56.6 million WordPress blogs in existence worldwide. According to critics and other bloggers, Blogger is the most popular blogging service used today. Promoting library's services, resources, and programmes online become a lot of easier with the help of a blog. Library blog's can be very effective tools for reaching online.

Blogs have become a very popular, easy and social platform to exchange information, and gradually are becoming a more acceptable reference sources even in peer reviewed publications. Service can be providing effectively through the blogs. In this connection, specialization of the blogs plays a crucial role in timeliness, perfection, and accuracy of blogs. Specialization saves the time of the users while searching through massive amount of uncontrolled information if every field is mixed up. Specialization is a best way to optimize the potential use of blogs if they are provided through non-conventional library services and information delivery

Webblog : The term "weblog" was coined by Jorn Barger on 17 December 1997. The short form, "blog," was coined by Peter Merholz, who jokingly broke the word weblog into the phrase weblog in the sidebar of his blog Peterme.com in April or May 1999. Thereafter, Evan Williams at Pyra Labs used "blog" as both a noun and verb ("to blog," meaning "to edit one's weblog or to post to one's weblog") and devised the term "blogger" in connection with Pyra Labs' Blogger product, leading to the popularization of the terms with no serious fact-checking.

Definition of Blog : Basically blog is defined as "a personal website or web page on which an individual records opinions, links to other sites, etc. on a regular basis add new material to or regularly update a blog: it's about a week since I last blogged with object write about (an event, situation, topic, etc.) in a blog blogged the Democratic and Republican national conventions as an independent".

Bolg Title : Title of the Bolg as title in general a name of the blog which we can understand the area of the Blog Address: Blog address in which bolg web sites as it is www.vaidyanathcollegelibrary.blogspot.com

Blogger's code of conduct

Blogger's code of conduct Tim O'Reilly for bloggers to enforce civility on their blogs by being civil them and moderating comments on their blogs. The idea of the code was first reported by BBC News, who quoted O'Reilly saying, "I do think we need some code of conduct around what is acceptable behavior, I would hope that it doesn't come through any kind of regulation it would come through self-regulation.

O'Reilly and others came up with a list of seven proposed ideas:

1. Take responsibility not just for your own words, but for the comments you allow on your blog.
2. Label your tolerance level for abusive comments.
3. Consider eliminating anonymous comments.
4. Ignore the Troll.

5. Take the conversation offline, and talk directly, or find an intermediary who can do so.
6. If you know someone who is behaving badly, tell them so.
7. Don't say anything online that you wouldn't say in person.

Blogger Guide : www.blogger .com explains following blogger guide:

Customize your blog's template : Blogger can customize blog template by his choice. On the blog various types of templates option are suggested to apply. Blogger can choose one and can apply.

Share your blog to Google+ : Created Blog can connect with or share with Google + and update automatically online.

Make money with your blog : Blogger can make money by placing the online advertisements on the blog. Number of user hints and usefulness of the blog decides user community.

Set up your custom domain : user can customize domain name of the blog and can set up the domain name and title name of the Blog.

Set your privacy options : Blogger can set up his privacy options and security for blog.

- Blogger can use upgraded interface.
- Blogger can enable dynamic views.
- Webmaster Tools to update the Blog.

Characteristics of Blog

1. **Online journal :** Blog is online journal that save valuable information online.
2. **Chronological :** Blog show the day to day information chronologically.
3. **Free software :** Blog is a free software

4. **Easily editable :** Blog content and comments can be easily edited by administrator or blogger and hence the blog is more useful in information exchange.
5. **Links and images :** One can give linkages to other e-resources and save the time to go separate website blog can directly link to other blog.
6. **Current content :** We can publish current content on the blog and inform to our user by online content update
7. **Multiple authors :** blog can publish by multiple authors, but main author edit and read.
8. **Online book discussion :** Blogger can open for online blog discussion. So any one can comment and give book reviews on the book.
9. **New releases :** books, video, electronic resources: libraries can display newly updated books in the library as well as E-Books and journals content.
10. **Upcoming events :** Library upcoming events like library weeks, Essay Competition, Book talk etc.
11. **Updating community :** Flash daily news on Blog to update our library communities which are connected to library blog.
12. **Appeal to special interest groups :** Library blogs can give appeal or instruction form the blogs for interest group.

Function as Marketing of library services

1. Promoting Library Services
2. Supporting Users
3. Community Engagements
4. Other Application of Blogs in Libraries:
5. Current Awareness Services, Selective Dissemination Information.

6. To highlight news or resources of interest
7. To post book reviews from student, faculty and staff members
8. To announce new acquisition in Library
9. To use as Library newsletter
10. To use as reference desk
11. To use as Libraries consortia

TYPES OF BLOGS

There are many different types of blogs, differing not only in the type of content, but also in the way that content is delivered or written on Wikipedia free encyclopedia as following.

1. Personal blogs : The personal blog is an ongoing diary or commentary written by an individual.

2. Microblogging : Micro blogging is the practice of posting small pieces of digital content—which could be text, pictures, links, short videos, or other media—on the Internet. Micro blogging offers a portable communication mode that feels organic and spontaneous to many and has captured the public imagination. Friends use it to keep in touch, business associates use it to coordinate meetings or share useful resources, and celebrities and politicians (or their publicists) micro blog about concert dates, lectures, book releases, or tour schedules. A wide and growing range of add-on tools enables sophisticated updates and interaction with other applications and the resulting profusion of functionality is helping to define new possibilities for this type of communication. Examples of these include Facebook and Tumblr.

3. Corporate and organizational blogs : A blog can be private, as in most cases, or it can be for business purposes. Blogs used internally to enhance the communication and culture in a corporation or externally for marketing, branding or public relations purposes are called corporate blogs. Similar blogs for clubs and societies are called club blogs, group blogs, or by similar names; typical use is to inform members and other interested parties of club and member activities.

4. Generation Types : Some blogs focus on a particular subject, such as

i. Political blogs:

ii. Health blogs,

iii. Travel blogs: (also known as travelogs)

iv. Gardening blogs,

v. House blogs,

vi. Fashion blogs,

vii. Project blogs,

viii. Education blogs,

ix. Niche blogs,

x. Classical music blogs,

xi. Quizzing blogs

xii. Legal Blogs (often referred to as a blawgs) or dreamlogs. Two common types of generation blogs are Art blog and Music blogs.

5. Blog by Type of Media : A blog comprising videos is called a vlog, one comprising links is called a Linklog a site containing a portfolio of sketches is called a Sketchblog or one comprising a photo is called a Photoblog. Blogs with shorter posts and mixed media types are called Tumbelogs. Blogs that are written on typewriters and then scanned are called typecast or typecast blogs.

6. Blog Types by devices : Blogs can also be defined by which type of device is used to compose it. A blog written by a Mobile device like a mobile phone or Personal Digital Assistant could be called a Moblogs. One early blog was

Wearable Wireless Webcam, an online shared diary of a person's personal life combining text, video, and pictures transmitted live from a wearable computer and EyeTap device to a web site. This practice of semi-automated blogging with live video together with text was referred to as surveillance. Such journals have been used as evidence in legal matters.

7. Reverse Blog : A Reverse Blog is composed by its users rather than a single blogger. This system has the characteristics of a blog, and the writing of several authors. These can be written by several contributing authors on a topic, or opened up for anyone to write. There is typically some limit to the number of entries to keep it from operating like a Web Forum.

8. The Blogosphere : The collective community of all blogs is known as the blogosphere. Since all blogs are on the internet by definition, they may be seen as interconnected and socially networked, through Blog rolls, comments, link backs refbacks, trackbacks or pingbacks and back links. Discussions "in the blogosphere" are occasionally used by the media as a gauge of public opinion on various issues. Because new, untapped communities of bloggers and their readers can emerge in the space of a few years, Internet marketers pay close attention to "trends in the blogosphere".

9. Blogging and advertising : It is common for blogs to feature advertisements either to financially benefit the blogger or to promote the blogger's favorite causes. The popularity of blogs has also given rise to "fake blogs" in which a company will create a fictional blog as a marketing tool to promote a product.

10. Popularity : Researchers have analyzed the dynamics of how blogs become popular. There are essentially two measures of this: popularity through citations, as well as popularity through affiliation (i.e., Blog roll). The basic conclusion from studies of the structure of blogs is that while it takes time for a blog to become popular through blog rolls, permalinks can boost popularity more quickly, and are perhaps more indicative of popularity and authority than Blog rolls, since they denote that people are actually reading the blog's content and deem it valuable or noteworthy in specific cases.

Blog Use In library

Blog can be use in library as following types.

1. News : Library can flash news about current happenings about the library. Events

2. Reviews : Books reviews about the new books arrived in the library

3. Comments : User can give comments about the posting or information published on blog.

4. What's new : Blog can show the feature what's new and publish the information newly available in library. What's new section on the blog is much important for the new arrival list new journals added and other functions.

5. Informational : Two ways interaction about the user and library is much strong inter communication that exchange the information useful to library users.

6. Discussion : Web 2.0 is two way discussions for interaction and can discuss on research topic on specific area.

7. Basically, your own website : you can post your videos, podcasts, pictures, and personal information all to one spot

8. Keeps patrons up–to-date Blogs are updated regularly, if not everyday

9. Allows for patrons to comment

10. Participation and community interest is most important while blogging.

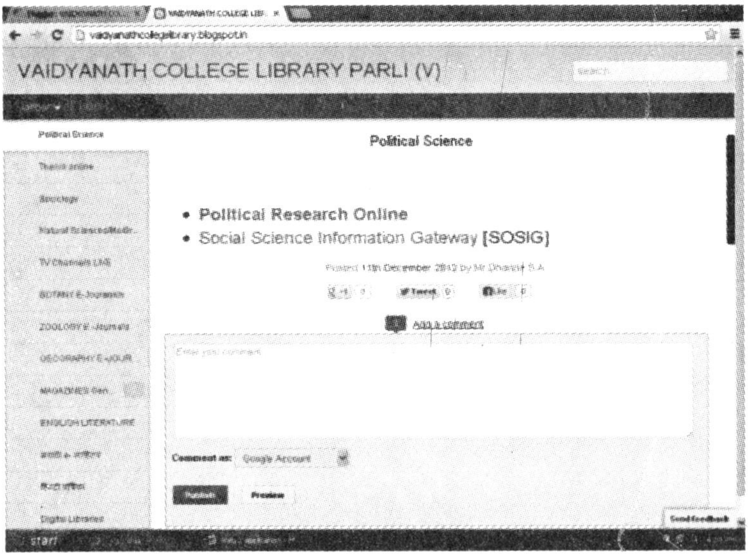

Fig. 7. Vaidyanath College Library Blog: http:// www.vaidyanathcollegelibrary.blogspot.com

11. Multiple Blogs for differing purposes : User can create multiple blogs for different function like Journal, E books, thesis, Reviews, Instant Messaging, current contents.

12. Update frequently : Blog can update frequently and serves updated information to its community and blogger.

13. Feedback to the library's Director : Blogger can allow feedback to librarian what types of comments are coming by user community.

14. Updates about new building
15. Inclusive (Children, Teens, Readers, Viewers)
16. Connection to their Community

FACE BOOK

These days' library and librarian are connecting through Facebook and sharing thoughts and ideas. It effects on the future development and strategy of developing the library discipline and other restricted barriers from librarian community. As well share other social issues and exchange comments from the community. So, Facebook is very popular tool in the library community. To set up library profile library services and facility e resources linking, e-books, e-journals, important pictures sharing all these resources. And create new group connect to our friends and share our views and difficulties and life moments. At the outset of the LASSIE project in March 2007, Facebook, the social networking site was considerably less well known than it is now (January 2008). Largely due to extensive media coverage in the UK, Facebook became extremely popular during the summer of 2007.

The history of Facebook is well documented on Wikipedia (Wikipedia: Facebook: http://en.wikipedia.org/wiki/Facebook) which tells how the site was launched in 2004 by a Harvard graduate. Initially membership was restricted to Harvard; however it was quickly extended to several other US universities. By 2005 anyone with university e-mail address was able to join and in September 2006 the site was opened up to anyone over the age of 13. By the end of 2007 the site was reported to have over 60 million users, being most popular in the UK, US and Canada. The largest network on Facebook is the London network which has over 2 million users.

Facebook use in Library : As with other social networking sites, you must register before starting to use Facebook. Facebook originally required a valid e-mail address for registration. The name of the institution in the e-mail address you provide at registration (e.g., the "vym" in xxxx@nyu.edu) still plays a significant role in your Facebook activities. To do library outreach to students, you must belong to the same "network" that they do. Your network is determined by the institutional name in your registered e-mail address; therefore, the e-mail address you use to register must contain the same institution name as those of the students you will be contacting. Network members can view the profiles of other members and send messages to them if their privacy preferences allow it. After registering, you create a profile. This is a page of information about you. You can only have one profile in Facebook and, as mentioned above, profiles must be associated with a person, not an institution creating a profile is a straightforward process that consists of filling out a series of forms. These forms are categorized under tabs labeled Basic, Contact, Personal, Work, Education, and Courses. The Work tab has a free-text Description field, useful for entering a statement about your role in your library. There is also a tab for adding a photo and one that explains how to drag and drop items in your profile to change the default layout. The amount of information you can provide in the profile, particularly of a personal nature, is considerable. When the profile page is displayed, it does not show the fields you left blank. Library 2.0: Taking the Library to Users. Face books is where college students today are doing much of their communication with one another. This makes it a natural choice as a medium for use by others wanting to reach them.

1. Librarians are creating Apps for catalog search and reference help.
2. Libraries are setting up profiles to attract users.
3. Librarians are using it for discussion and work within the profession.

Like following figure of the MMU library services face book page which is exposed like library website, which they shown views of the library and library services, infrastructure and facilities for the users.

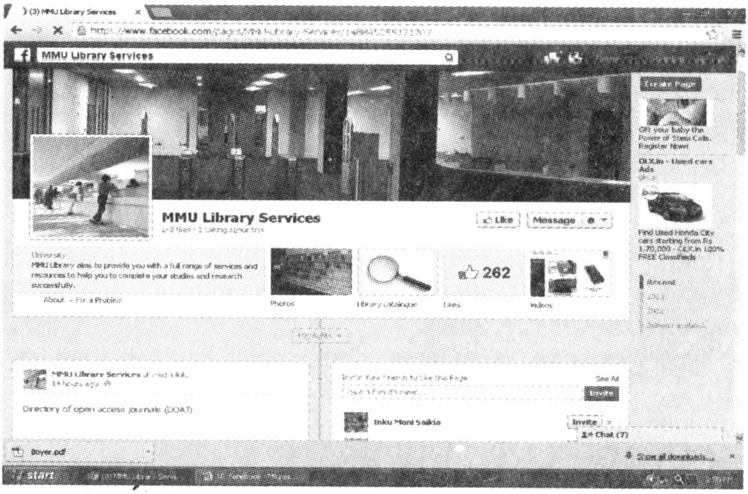

Fig. 8. MMU Library Websites, http://www.facebook.com

Facebook Applications (Apps) for Libraries

There are several library-related Facebook applications that have been developed recently. Some of them are useful o librarian for their day to day library work as we display in following figure of facebook.

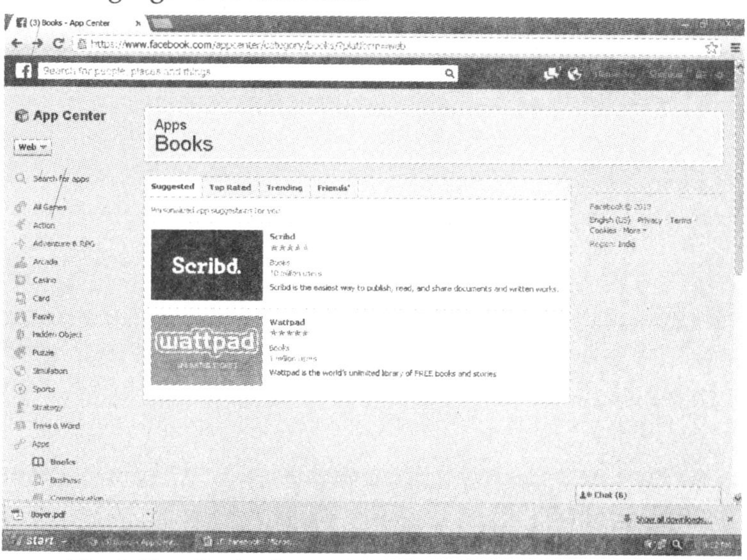

Fig. 9. Face Books Apps Center/http://www.facebook.com

Below is a list of some of these, but further details can also be found in the Facebook. Group about Library Applications useful posting on the Top Facebook Applications for Libraries Jane Secker (2008) stated that in his paper as following.

1. JSTOR Search

One can search JSTOR from within Facebook. A link to JSTOR can include in your profile, and can update it regularly.

2. LibGuides Librarian

If your library uses spring share's LibGuides subject guides maker for libraries (http://demo.libguides.com/), this application allows you to display your guides in your Facebook profile and also provides a search of your library's catalogue.

3. Facebook Librarian

This application is essentially a virtual librarian service which provides links to books and other resources. There is also an "Ask a Librarian" service which means you can list yourself as a librarian and be available to answer queries.

4. Books iRead

This application is evidently the most popular book application on Facebook and it lets you share a virtual bookshelf of titles you are currently reading, those you want to read, those you have read in the past, and books you won't read. You can also rate titles and list books you own as well as highlight your favorite books. You can also check out your friends' reads, and view new books added to the quickly-growing collection of 2.8 million books.

5. Bookshare

This is a similar book sharing application that allows you to list books that you own, like or love. You can rate books, add reviews and mark books are being available to borrow by others. Various Library Catalogues are available for searching from within Facebook including:

6. COPAC Search

One can use ability to search the union catalogue COPAC within Facebook. A link to COPAC is included on your profile.

7. European Library Search

User can search European Library Website while using the Facebook.

8. World Cat Search

Like any search worldcat search also user get bibliographic information on the above search.

9. UIUC Library catalog

This application allows you to search the library catalogue of the University of Illinois at Urbana– Champaign or request live assistance from a librarian.

While Using Facebook Librarian Must Think As Following:

- If you decide to take the plunge and sign up for a Facebook account do spend some time reading up on the security and privacy settings relating to your account. The default option is to have your profile open which means anyone (including non-Facebook users) can view it.
- Make sure you are happy (and understand) the security settings you have saved. We would recommend you only have your profile available to your friends and not to everyone on your network.
- Be careful about adding too much personal information to your profile, such as your full date of birth or home address for obvious security reasons and also keep in your mind the idea of your profile as a public space,

as this will help you to decide what is appropriate and not appropriate to add to it.

- Only share information on Facebook you are really comfortable with work colleagues knowing, as inevitably they will become your 'friends'.
- Add some applications, (including some of the above listed library related apps) to your profile, but be selective about what you add or your profile can soon become overwhelming.
- Also consider that each app has separate terms and conditions that must be agreed to.
- Spend time building up your friends network on Facebook. It's possible to search for people in various ways and you can import e-mail contact lists to see who might be already on Facebook.
- Be selective about who you accept as a friend, so don't accept requests from people you really don't know, but also do remember that the more friends you have on Facebook the more useful it can become.
- Join your local network and join some groups of interest. It's worthwhile searching for groups that already exist and relate to libraries or professional interests you might have.
- Consider setting up a group or a page to experiment with how these features works – they can provide additional publicity for any professional groups you are involved in and may prove to be useful in promoting library services in the future.
- Limit the amount of time you spend on Facebook so it doesn't become an addiction.

TWITTER

Fig. 10. Twitter logo http://www.twitter.com

Twitter lets people send and receive short messages (called Tweets) via the web or via SMS using a mobile phone. Messages on Twitter are limited to a maximum of 140 characters, including spaces, and they're generally public. Because each message is just a sentence or two, a carefully crafted post can convey a good deal of information without taking a lot of time to read or write. In addition, because Twitter has millions of users, it's a good place to find and connect with people interested in your institution and your areas of expertise.

To automatically see what someone else is saying, you "follow" them. Those who regularly receive your posts are your "followers." You don't need to give each other permission to follow, and you can view Tweets without signing into Twitter, but you must sign in to follow someone. Example, a library could share all kinds of news that patrons want. Short messages can tell people about events such as readings, lectures, and book sales; newly available resources; or changes in the building hours. One message a day or one a week could share a tip on finding or accessing information online or in the building. Twitter posts can link to interesting news stories about literacy or about libraries. Twitter is one name that has grown in leaps and bounds in terms of use, membership, and popularity. This social platform has achieved worldwide popularity with an approximately 225 million users, and generating as much as 340 million tweets in a day! In this post, we are going to learn about some fun facts associated with this micro-blogging platform. The story behind the inception of Twitter is pretty interesting. According to Jack Dorsey The board members of the podcasting organization, Odeo gathered for a day-long brainstorming session in a park, and being seated on a kid's slide munching Mexican delicacies that the idea of utilizing an SMS service to interact with a small group was introduced.

LIBRARIES ON TWITTER

Twitter gives a new opportunity to share information not just with their internal clients but also with people outside the institution, who are interested in their topics. Since people often look to see who a Twittering person or institution is following libraries, can add resources to the list of accounts they follow.

1. http://twitter.com/adalib), Ada Library in Boise, Idaho and http://twitter.com/Cleveland_PL Cleveland Public Library use Twitter to point out highlights on their websites—everything from exhibit announcements, to links for nominating "your favorite librarian," to holiday hours.
2. The Missouri River Regional Library (http://twitter.com/mrrl) posts information about teen events and recently linked to research about the value of libraries in lean economic times.
3. The Glendale (Ariz.) Public Library (http://twitter.com/GlendaleLibrary) Tweets about its programs.
4. (http://twitter.com/askundergrad), The Undergraduate Library at the University of Illinois–Urbana-Champaign use for example, lets students know about upcoming deadlines issue books ("5 days left to return

ALL media items"), service issues

5. (http://twitter.com/yalescilib) The Yale University Science Libraries announce workshops on library resources, provide links to online archives, and give tips on sending text messages to a librarian.
6. http://twitter.com/NCSUEngLibrary) North Carolina State University Engineering Library links to both university and external blog posts.
7. (http://twitter.com/LPI_Library), The Lunar and Planetary Institute Library for instance, has linked to the Carnival of Space blog, the International Year of Astronomy Discovery Guide, and a report on the National Science Digital Library (NSDL) meeting
8. (http://twitter.com/BL_Ref_Service) British library reference service is a team of information professionals. They are delivering services to reading rooms and beyond. Library reference service is for readers as shown in following figure.

Fig. 11. Reference Services on Twitter: http://twitter.com/BL_Ref_Service

9. (http://twitter.com/NPCLibrary) The National Press Club does a nice job of combining announcements of coming events with URLs and some personal observations.
10. (http://twitter.com/LibraryJournal : as Twitter is way to transfer quick message to its community following types of JSTOR leading journals publication are on twitter to provide publication update and to update authors and others connected people.

Fig. 12. Journals update on twitter: http://twitter.com/jstor

11. **http://twitter.com/alaannual:** twitter is use by ALA annual, to spread message about annual conference and exhibition by ALA as following.

Fig. 13. Conference Seminar update on twitter http://twitter.com/alaannual

12. **To search Jobs http://twitter.com/ALA_JobLIST:** Twitter is best way to find jobs suitable update. Following figure shows that service by ALA_JobLIST. These types of accounts show the new job notifications and job search tips and strategies to user community. So the twitter is use to search the jobs.

Fig. 14. ALA JOB alert on twitter: http: // twitter.com/ALA_JobLIST

Also, the local newspaper, national and international news sources such as NPR (http://twitter.com/NPR) and BBC (http://twitter.com/BBC), and professional information sources are all good candidates to follow. Therefore these are only example library web sites but it is not limited those library, so many libraries are using the twitter applications to communicate the library functions. The best known microblogging services are Twitter, Tumblr, Pownce, and Jaiku. I have described some pragmatic issues about Twitter as information tool, based on some of my own experimentation and citation on twitter. Reference services in libraries People could "follow" a twitter account to learn about library events, new books, or get responses to library user questions.

Positive Impact on Education

Gabriela Grosseck and Carmen Holotescu stated that twitter can have a positive impact on educational factors due to some **good points** as follows:

1. engaging education and sharing the best practices that a teacher is using in his/her classroom
2. it changes classroom dynamics
3. very useful to get helpful information
4. it can serve both as a means of analysis and an object of analysis
5. it connects people that one would not have met otherwise
6. it keep track of a conversation students carry on a particular topic
7. it's fun and gives students more insight into what's really going on in courses
8. it's a good way of making a quick announcement
9. Exploring the language that students have used in the session, that other people would naturally use to describe an event's probability.
10. being limited to just 140 characters really focuses the attention, it's developed its own sort of discursive grammar set, requiring a great deal of summarizing (even synthesizing, on occasion)
11. may be useful for our professional development and building a true educational community
12. teachers are connecting their students to the real world
13. it gives the students a sense of what a person is like outside of the classroom (they end up being a lot more comfortable with classroom discourse)
14. make us feel nice about being human (quieter students can be heard)

15. it provide age-appropriate environments
16. students use Twitter as a tool that supports reflection
17. Twitter is microblogging which many times is much more efficient than RSS feeds [Davis, 2008]
18. Twitter is purposefulness, curriculum-centred but not curriculum-bound
19. The teacher can post lecture notes.
20. Library community: Twittering in Library or outside of it is about learning.
21. Exploring collaborative writing: it promotes writing as a fun activity, it fosters editing skills develop literacy skills; it can give our students a chance to record their cognitive trails and then use them to reflect on their work.
22. Reader response: students can use tweets to send out questions and observations to the group while engaged in college activities.
23. Explore the potential of microblogging in formal and informal settings: Twitter linked to a course/class blog can offer our students opportunities to discuss different kinds of online discourse, considering voice, purpose, audience, to organize ideas, reflect, send notes, manage meet-ups, unexpected discovery etc.
24. Collaboration across schools, countries for example, students leave phone-tweets as they come across real-world examples of what they are studying in class or as they conduct fieldwork.
25. **Project Management :** if you set up a group working on a project the tweets can be picked up on cell phones (as can email).
26. A tool for assessing opinion, examining consensus, looking for outlying ideas. Twitter also could be used in an academic setting to foster interaction about a given topic.

WIKIS

Introduction : Wikis, like blog it is means of publishing to the web that again dispense with the need for dedicated web publishing software. The wikis support the relation of full scale website with its combination of templates, authoring tools and audit trails. In wikis user can add, edit, change and improve on existing content with use of collaborative editing the Wikis. This is online webpage for library that can be easily editable and give multiple accesses all over world. Website library websites can be created by the WIKIS librarian can put library information on the wikis and can give linkages to website.

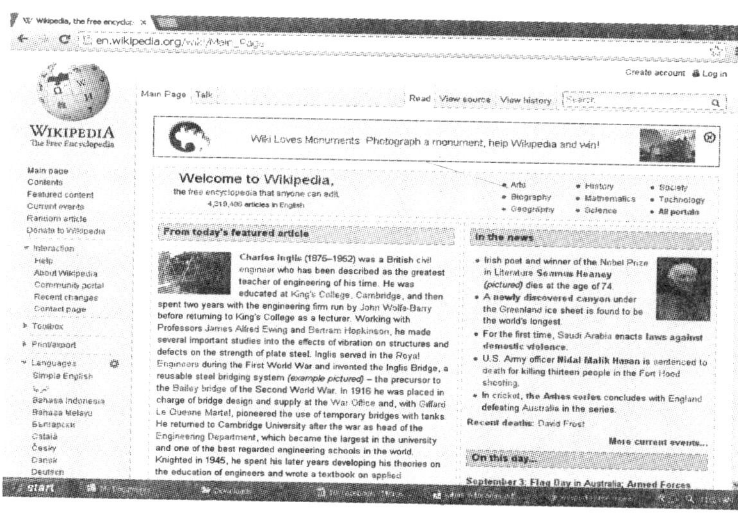

Fig. 15. Wikipedia Home page, http://www.wikipedia.org/wiki/main.page

What is Wikis?

A wiki is a simple yet powerful web based collaborative way of for content creation and editing content. It can anyone add new article or revise or edit existing files. It is way for researcher, student and for collaborative work and information storage and dissemination works.

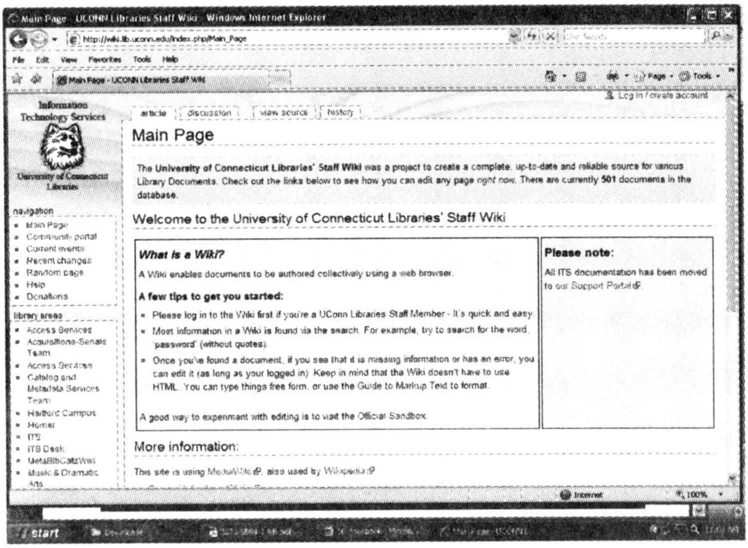

Fig. 16. Library Staff information wikis: http://wiki.lib.uconn.edu/index.php/Main_Page

Wikis Characteristics : following are some basic characteristics of wikis as tools of web 2.0 tools. Therefore the following characteristics are important and simple to understand the impact of wikis on education and libraries.

- **Collective memory :** Wikis has characteristics of collective memory. It has creation collaboration of many hand and talents. so it is collective memory.
- **Good for writing down ideas :** It is good way to write down our ideas and views about the existing ideas and information. Also anyone can add the ideas and views to discover new ideas.
- **Instantly collaborative :** As we seen collective memory of people it means it is collaborative. Wikis is instantly collaborative for researcher and information worker.
  a. Collaboration among libraries (extra-organizational)

b. Collaboration among library staff (intra-organizational)

c. Collaboration among library staff and patrons

d. Collaboration among patrons

- **Accessible from anywhere :** Wikis is online web 2.0 tools so it has online accessible tools. So therefore wherever Internet browser is accessible wikis also are available to work anywhere.
- **Paperless :** To save nature is similar to save life, now it necessary every person to save the papers and jungles which are importance for creation of papers. Wikis are working with paperless mission.
- **Intranet :** Internet is networks of network. Intranet is network of small group of network like institutional network. So wikis can work on Intranet based network and can collaborate and work on the Intranet.
- **Staff/User manual :** Wikis are useful tools for most important tools to information collection, dissemination and retrieval of information. So user manuals to inform library users. Also staff manuals to inform fem staff on web is possible by the wikis.
- **Encyclopaedia :** It is world's knowledge store house and everyone can put knowledge and information on wikis. Wikipedia is free encyclopaedia and wiki any one can freely add information and can edit.
- **Subject guides :** Wikis are important for creating subject guides. Every subject in the world it has specific concept and ideas. Characteristic about subject guides in wikis are basic in the wikis.
- **Wikibooks :** It is tools in wikis to subject wise books classification and information about the books. New subject and new books can add by authors and readers to read out the books.

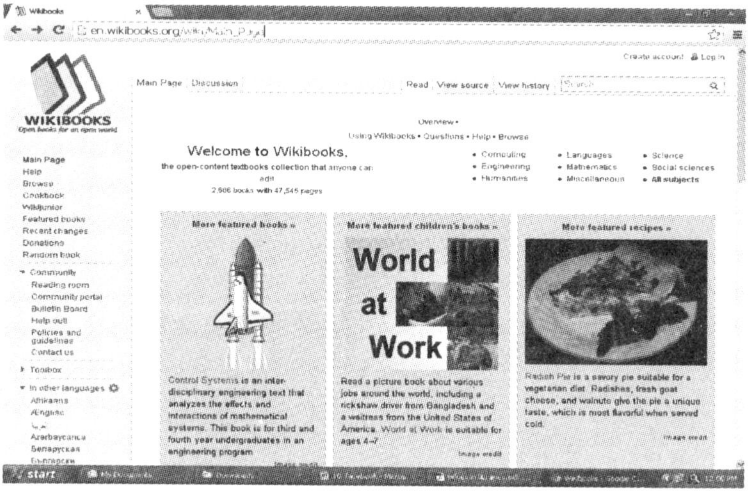

Fig. 9. Wiki books http://en.wikibooks.org/wiki/

Following figure of wikibooks is show the way of subject social science subjects and available wiki books in the subjects. In the social science anthropologies, communication economics, education geography, law, political science, psychology and sociology are basic subject and books like in the library science application ICT in libraries etc.

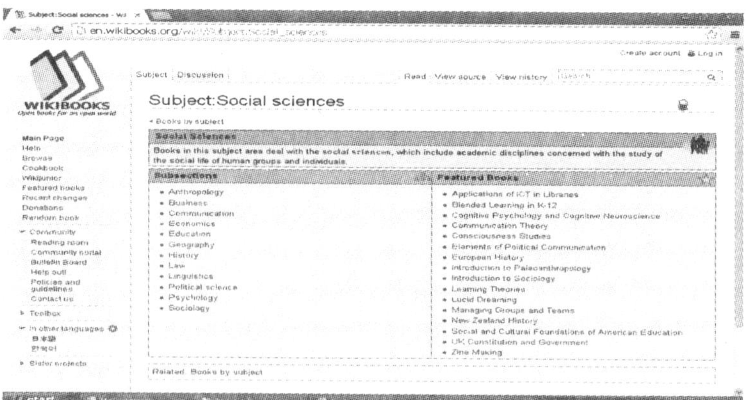

Fig. 10. Wiki books on Social Science: http://en.wikibooks.org/wiki/Subject:Social_sciences

Wikis as Resource Reviews Collections : Wikis can also be used as resource reviews collections. For example, what the Butler University Libraries are doing with Seed wiki. They have over 130 Reviews of databases, books, websites, and style guides that are part of their Reference collection. And librarians are using them for best practices collections, such as on the library success wiki; also the library instruction wiki is a collection of all the best resources for instructional librarians, etc. So, to search & easily updatable resource for patrons which anyone can edit wikis.

Wikis for Event Planning : Beyond strictly academic – library organizations are using them for conference planning – an informal space to have information about speakers' and attendees schedules, dining information, tagging and twitter information. Web page, Editable, Multiple authors, Server or hosted, Free or cost, Links and images.

Wikiquote : Wikis is also has collection of quote on all great peoples all over the world. Wikiquotes figure shown as following those Gautma Buddhas quotations Dhammapada and tripithakas quotations collection are as follow.

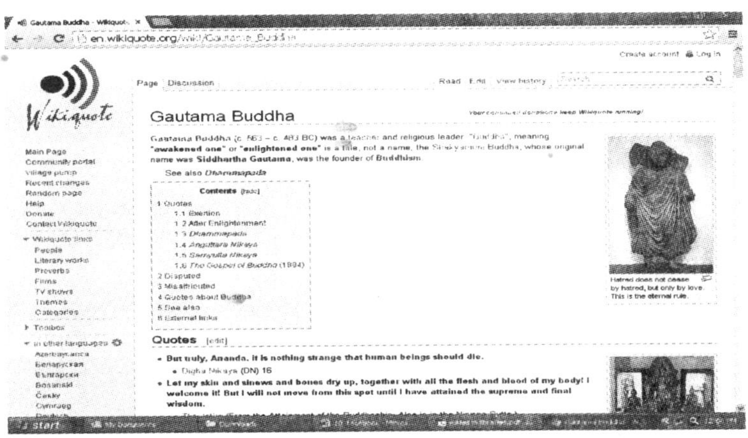

Fig. 11. Wikiquote on Wikipedia Gautama Buddha quotation page

I. Other Uses of Wikis in Libraries:

- **A library website or individual departments :** any one can create use of wiki as individual website or any library website freely.
- **Book Reviews :** Library can put book list and its reviews to user community.
- **Book clubs & discussions :** Web 2.0 is two way interactions between user and receiver so it enhances the online discussion, or to create Book clubs.
- **Education & Training – 2.0 :** Online training and education we can perform by the Library.
- **History of the library and community :** Library success a best practices wiki is an example for the use of wikis in libraries. History of the library community and function of the library community can display on the wikis to know the importance in the society.

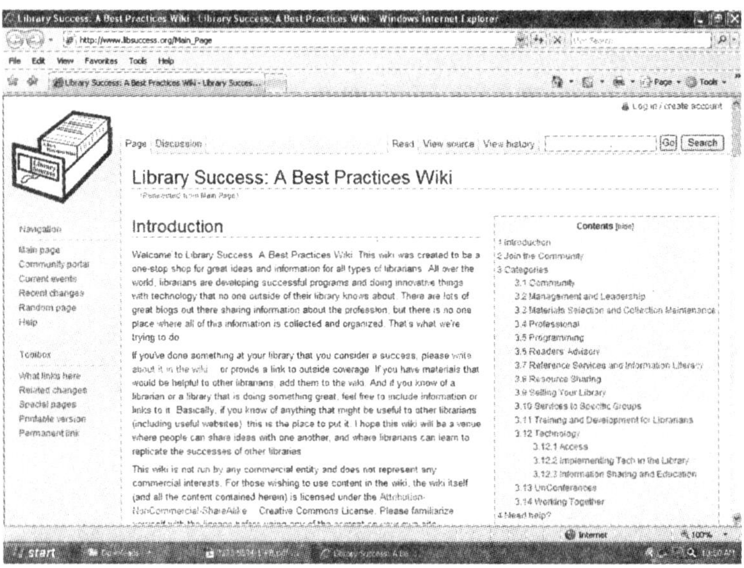

Fig. 12. Library Success: A Best Practices wiki (http: //www. libsuccess.org/)

PODCASTING AND VODCASTING

Introduction : Web 2.0 technologies comprise an array of web enabled services which are used for diverse purpose. Podcasting is one of the web 2.0 applications, which enhances the new ways of information communication, especially content information. It is used in web 2.0 for broadcasting audio. A synonymous term such as audiocasting, audioblogging and webcasting are used for podcasting. Vodcasting, on the other hand consist of video is very popular by sites like google and you tube. According to Wikipedia "podcasting" term was used for the first time by Ben Hammersley, a journalist, in his article "the Guardian" on February 12, 2004. Podcasting gives. Libraries and other information provider groups are now using the podcasting in services. To create, edit and disseminating podcast or information content there is new opportunity for library and information professional.

Podcast is an audio file made available on internet. It is a combination of two words broadcasting and Ipod. The podacasting technology, audio is syndicated, though RSS feed that was adopted form blog, that can be download by new contents of updated podcast. Podcast can be download and listen any MP3 format supported media player or on personal computers and also on CD'S DVD players.

How work Podcasting

A podcaster records and edit using suitable software and produces an audio file often in MP3 format that many contain lectures, interview unlike e-mail and Web.

Podcasts and Vodcasts : Podcasts are files that are gradually replacing the old-fashioned, static Web recordings. Vodcasts, or Vid-eocasts, are relatively new, and offer video content. As broadband access becomes more readily available, vodcasts will surely gain momentum in the near fu-ture.

Use of Podcasting in Library : Kaushik Anna (June 2010) stated in his article podcasting in library environment as following.

1. **Library Web site :** there many websites contain podcasts on various subjects periodically that updated on website.
2. **Library website with podcast :** So many websites have podcast videos for users to give new announcement of clip of the important message.
3. **Podcast with Database :** Emerald management reviews named reviews is updating monthly on emerald management publishing database.
4. **Podcast with Journals :** Podcast is now useful in Journals that can be access in audio format and can be link via RSS this example is journal first Monday on web (http: //www.firstmondaypodcast.org
5. **Podcast on Blog :** Podcast in the form of Interview important statements and books discussion, current happenings library training, virtual tours etc. audio and video can link on blog.

Podomatic : It is an example of web collection of podcast clips on one platforms like subjects, Arts Business, Comedy, Education, Games Hobbies, News, Medicine, Music, Sports, TVfims, Technology, Literature, Food and other.

Fig. 21. PODOMATIC http://www.podomatic.com/directory

Benefits in Library

1. Podcasting can be available anywhere online, so it is useful to disseminate information. It is interactive learning tools for remote user.
2. It requires minimum hardware and software and so it is cost effective for library.
3. It is portable and enables users to carry and access without much peripherals also can use on Mobile.
4. Repeated listening and flexibility enables users to get better understanding and control on information.
5. It saves time of user and collect data in audiovisual form.

SOCIAL BOOKMARKING

Introduction : Social bookmarking has developed as a social software tool that allows users to submit, classify, localise and share their bookmarked web pages to a central site where they can be located and 'tagged' by other users. It is a process that is used by people to organise, arrange, maintain and reserve links on website pages. Tags then provide the user the ability to insert keywords to distribute content to other sites on the internet (Dixon). Social bookmarking can be used as a knowledge management system for individuals and groups. It is a powerful research and annotation tool that is searchable, shareable, and accessible from any computer. Social Bookmarking tools are excellent resource discovery tools; when searching for a particular subject, users may see that other users tagged a particular web page and other sites under similar tags. This allows users to see the collective list of resources from all the users who share the same research apparent; these tools are web-based and searchable. And they facilitate the development of communities of interest and expertise (Barsky & Purdon, 2006)

Definition

"Social bookmarking is the practice of saving bookmarks to a public Web site and "tagging" them with keywords."

History

History of Social Bookmarking we have to go back to 1996 with the launch of the website itLists.com, this was the first site to utilize the concept of shared bookmarks. After few years this idea was followed by companies such as Backflip, Blink, Clip2, Hotlinks and Quiver. These companies however failed to make an impact on the market due to the dot.com crash of 2001. Therefore we wait until 2003 when del.icio.us launched its own tag related social bookmarking site. In a short space of time del.icio.us expanded very quickly, this led to other companies following their lead. In the next few years's websites such as Simpy, Furl, Stumbleupon, Netvouz, Diigo, Digg, reddit, Newsvine joined the fray and expanded on the principles of social bookmarking. Also in 2004, the social photo sharing website Flickr was released, and inspired by Delicious it soon added a tagging feature. In 2006, Magnolia later renamed to Gnolia, Blue Dot later renamed to Faves, Mister Wong, and Diigo entered the bookmarking field, and Connectbeam included a social bookmarking and tagging service aimed at businesses and enterprises. In 2007, IBM released its Lotus Connections product.

Advantages

Therefore some of the advantages of using social bookmarking tools stated by Dixon Angela in SVEA Training Module:

a. Easy to set-up and manage your account

b. It is available for public viewing rather than restricted to one personal computer.

c. It is possible to see what bookmarks are popular with other users.

d. Can significantly widen your available resources and allows you to form a community of like-minded users.

e. Tags or keywords can be used as descriptors for your bookmarks to make them really searchable.

f. Use as a networking tool to share good practice world-wide and closer to home.

g. Subscribe to someone's bookmarks via RSS

h. Develops a collection of reviewed and more importantly, approved sites for students to use.

i. Lists are easily downloadable and transferable between social bookmarking providers

j. A great learner centered discovery tool

k. Engages learners in collaborative activity

Disadvantages

a. Lacks authority control - no standard set of keywords/

tags/controlled vocabulary

b. Singular vs. plural

c. Spelling errors

d. Tags with more than one meaning (e.g. "bow" could mean ribbon, tie, prow of a ship, violin bow)

e. Limitations with interface (e.g. sorting, downloading)

f. Susceptible to corruption and collusion (spammers have started bookmarking a web page over and over again)

Social Bookmarking Work

Social bookmarking works discover webpage's tagging and sharing with community as following.

a. Discover web pages of interest by tag searches, friends, and serendipity

b. Add page to social bookmark site

c. Add tags to page with words chosen by the user to describe the page

d. Follow tags to discover other pages and users with the same interests

The Educational Benefits of Social Bookmarking

Recently, social bookmarking has become very popular in education. Many teachers complete and handout reading lists for students to use in assignments; this would be simplified and made more accessible by using a link to an online version of the teacher's preferred lists electronically through a social bookmarking site. Therefore student can use these reading lists any time and any where they wish.

Social Bookmarking Tips

It is very important to choose the tag wisely because the tags are mirror to search hyperlinked information. Therefore also Headlines should not like advertisement taglines. Headlines should include keywords. Username is indexed on search engines. Include bookmarking links in your web sites. Choose only potentially important information. Like above tips user can add and tag information very effectively for future use.

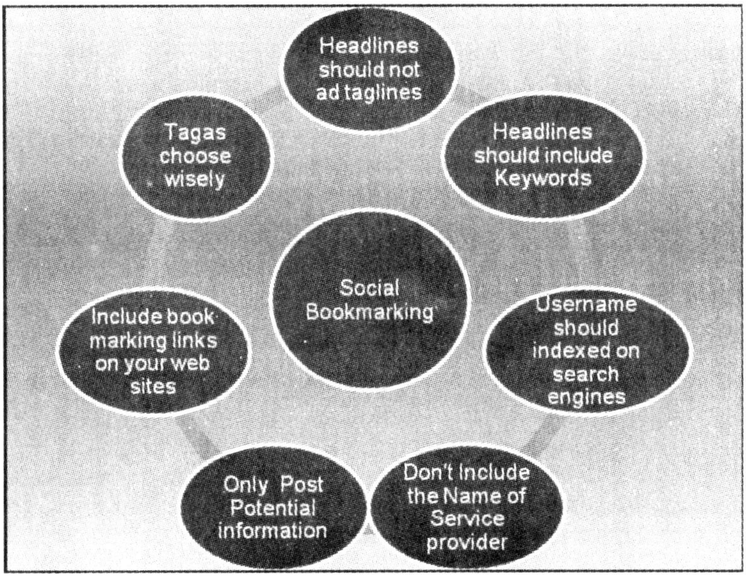

Fig. 22. Social Bookmarking tips

Evaluation Features

Social Book marking evaluate as following use of tools as:

a. **Shared and/or private :** It is necessary to know the social bookmarking sites are shared or private that decides the bookmarking sites futures views and developments.

b. **FAQ :** frequently asked questions are important for easy use and awareness among the user and necessary in evaluation.

c. Bookmarks (icons for toolbar that allows you to quickly bookmark and tag)

d. Tag Clouds (subject list) Tags clouds are important in

evaluation of social bookmarking sites. Depth in subject and keywords and heading in the subjects show the usefulness for user.

e. **RSS :** Whether are there linking with RSS for automatically update bookmarking.

f. **Blog :** Whether are there linking with Blogs for automatically update bookmarking.

g. **Open Source :** The social bookmarking is open source for the user.

h. **Import/Export :** Can user import information on the pages or exports to their personal use.

i. **Cost :** Coast is important while using the social; bookmarking. Is it free or associated with pay and use.

j. **Backup :** Important information we can share whether there is back for information.

How to Post bookmarks

a. Click "post"

b. Type in the URL (e.g. http://google.com)

c. Click "Save" button.

d. Type in a description (this is the title of your bookmark)

e. Type in notes regarding the site (optional)

f. Type in appropriate tags.

g. Decide to share or not share

h. Click "Save" button.

Social bookmarking tools

Tools for social bookmarking are as following some of them has described for their usefulness for students and community.

a. del.icio.us : http://www.delcious.com

b. Simpy : http://www.simpy.co/

c. Connotea : http:// www.connotea.org

d. CiteULike : http://citeulike.org, citeulike is a free service for managing and discovering scholarly references

e. Diigo: http://www.diigo.com

f. Digg: http://www.digg.com

Delicious

Delicious is one of the most used social bookmarking tools on the web. From primary through higher education, there is a place for delicious as part of delivering courses and supporting learners. It has a simple interface and intuitive features that are perfect for students of all levels and abilities. Delicious allows anyone to identify, classify and share useful websites. It allows the sites to be 'tagged' with key words that will make it easy for other users to find those sites. The key benefit is that teachers can make online resources accessible to learners wherever they log on. It also means that the learners can share new resources they have found with their fellow learners.

Diigo : Diigo is an abbreviation for the 'Digest of Internet Information, Groups and Other stuff'. In addition to the social bookmarking aspects, Diigo allows you to highlight parts of a webpage and attach sticky notes that can be either made private or public – perfect for class collaboration.

Features and Facts : Diigo is launched in 2006 for free information exchange and collaboration. It is free for users to create accounts on diigo. It has ability for users to highlight any part of a webpage and attach sticky notes on Diigo. It shares annotations and also different levels of privacy. It has customizable toolbars. This also automatically exports to delicious. Just as a student may highlight particular text in lecture notes or use sticky notes in books, Diigo has the advantage of doing this online. It encourages active e-reading and retention of information. Whilst other social bookmarking sites only save the link, Diigo can select, save and share text and pictures.

Social News Sites : Some social bookmarking sites are differentiated by the content that users add to their lists. A particular group is that of social news sites. They provide you with quick access to a variety of news articles, along with the opinions of other users. Articles and news from other websites are aggregated within the social news sites where, not only can you share content relevant to your interests; you can also participate in discussions with fellow users.

Digg : Digg is one of the most popular social news sites. Which is founded in 2004 and it is integrated with Facebook connect. Ii has specific category for the work. Digg has widget for the Blog and, it is USA based Social news sites tools update all news on one platform and has downloadable toolbars. Digg has mobile version as app for smart phone on (m.digg.com) a great feature of Digg is the ability to quickly view the top stories in the last 24 hours rated by the Digg community.

Use of Social bookmarking in Libraries

a. To collect and share sites for best practice
b. Create and maintain dynamic web pages/subject guides
c. Marketing/Promotion
d. Tag articles and web sites for specific classes

Tagging

Tagging essentially enables users to create subject headings for the object at hand. As tagging is essentially Web 2.0 because it allows users to add and change not only content (data), but content describing content (metadata). In Flickr, users tag pictures. In Library Thing, they tag books. In Library 2.0, users could tag the library's collection and thereby participate in the cataloging process.

Tagging simply makes lateral searching easier. The often-cited example of the U.S. Library of Congress's Subject Heading "cookery," which no English speaker would use when referring to "cookbooks," illustrates the problem of standardized classification. Tagging would turn the useless "cookery" to the useful "cookbooks" instantaneously, and lateral searching would be greatly facilitated. Of course, tags and standardized subjects are not mutually exclusive. The catalog of Library 2.0 would enable users to follow both standardized and user-tagged subjects; whichever makes most sense to them. In turn, they can add tags to resources. The user responds to the system, the system to the user. This tagged catalog is an open catalog, a customized, user-centered catalog. It is library science at its best

a. Tags are words that the user chooses that tell about the main points or subject of the webpage
b. Tags are used in many of the social networking, Web 2.0 programs.
c. Tags can be viewed by looking at tag clouds and tag bundles.
d. Tags may be put onto your own webpages or blogs.

CONCLUSIONS

There are many social bookmarking tools available for use within learning and teaching. Everyone has its value, with social networking sites such as Facebook having the functionality of social bookmarking. Now that we have been introduced to some of the popular ones, user can pick and choose which ones to use, by looking at the key features relevant to what you want to achieve.

INSTANT MESSAGING

Introduction

Instant messaging (IM) refers as virtual reference

service. Through this service librarians can handle user's enquiries instantly in a pre-defined time period and answers user's questions without wastage of time from a remote location. But application of this tool is found only in seven national libraries websites. *Instant Messaging for reference questions is becoming increasingly popular, especially at academic libraries, it show that student can directly contact to the librarian online*. Library of Congress, National Library of USA have instant messaging service for different section includes Newspapers/Periodicals, American Memory Historical Collections and Digital Reference Section. Instant messaging (IM) has become a popular communication method, especially among younger people who form a large part of the libraries users' population. Simply stated, IM is real-time online communication between two or more people. The medium enables people to .chat Via the Internet by rapidly ex changing text messages. One user chats with another user by typing a message into a specialized window, or chat room Generated by IM software. The message appears almost immediately on the other users screen. The recipient reads it and replies by typing a response. Only an Internet connection is required to access basic chat systems. Unlike e-mail and Web forms, IM is well fitting to conducting reference interviews, helpful questions, and receiving feedback.

Multi-protocol IM

Following figure show that Instant messaging can be soul for the current awareness services while use in the library. Connect library community by use of instant messaging technologies for better communication and solve every difficulty.

Fig. 23. Instant Messaging views: http://betanews.com/2013/04/30/ miranda-ng-is-a-multi-protocol-im-client-with-style/

Instant Messaging Technologies

There are number of technology available today. Most of them are free to download and easy to use such as, yahoo messenger, AOL messengers, Google talk, Skype and Windows live messengers. Others technology are cost associated and for business orientated like IBM SomeTime and Cisco Jabber.

Characteristics of Instant Messaging (IM)

a. Real-time

b. Casual

c. Multi-task

d. Free

e. Online messaging

f. Information service

g. Help at point of need

Steps for Setting up Instant Messaging Services, by (Marianne Foley 2002)

A. Selection of IM System and software includes

Software have to update with following features.

1. Support for AOL, MSN and Yahoo! IM services.
2. File transferring and sharing.
3. Support for group conversations.
4. Automated transcript saving.
5. Alerts for new IM messages and users.
6. Easy insertion of emotions and images.
7. Notification when the respondent is typing to answer an IM
8. Displaying connectivity to accounts in the system tray.

Fig. 24. http://www.businessproductivity.com/does-instant-messaging-in-the-workplace-increase-business-productivity/

B. Setting up IM Accounts

To set accounts on account on AOL, MSN and Yahoo

C. Staffing and Services

Librarians, reference staff, and student assistants monitor multiple reference services from a single service point in each library. There was concern that adding IM to these services might compromise the quality of walk-in, phone, and email reference transactions. However, assigning IM duties to staff outside of reference shifts would have been problematic due to staffing levels. At the service desks, multiple reference staff members are available at peak hours so we felt that they could absorb this additional service. On evenings and weekends, the service desks are covered by only one reference staff member.

D. Training

How to use abbreviation symbols in IM and chat speak training required to staff and user.

E. Webpage Creation

Ask librarian like web page with separate instruction and guideline is effective idea. Like following figure that can be very effective to staff as well as student.

The experiment with IM reference service may be considered a success, despite a few problems and some growing caution. Chat reference will not succeed the library other reference services, but it offers another way to reach and educate patrons.

ONLINE VIDEO

Online Video is mush important in the online information collection and Dissemination. Therefore online Videos on various subject, videos on YouTube various conceptual videos are free of cost available on You Tube. Search tools and can share all over world by this tools and so on this is much better for to share the information on internet. To share ideas and thought in the form of video it is better to use you tube clips on various topics. You tube have collection of videos no various subjects and current happenings in the society. One can use this tool to know the subject or some basic idea about subject in audiovisual form.

Fig. 25. YouTube video http://www.youtube.com

You Tube Function

- **Share video :** Every user can share video on the you tube, and can create account
- **Training :** How to share the videos and use the videos has given guidelines to use.
- **Promotion :** Promotion of various products and marketing is easy by using the you tube, Because YouTube is famous for its newly videos and archives collection. So most of the peoples are using the YouTube for promotions of the products.
- **Accessible :** Accessibility is not restricted to user for about downloading the videos and other information. For accessibility there are divisions as teen kids and adults.
- **Free :** YouTube is free for everyone to share upload and download educational as well as other informative videos freely.

Public Ideas for YouTube

- Contests – teens/kids/adults
- Local History
- Training & Teaching

YouTube use in library

Market upcoming events : You tube can market happenings in library, library weeks, books exhibition celebration of events and upcoming events. Marketing of these events can upload on you Tube and it shares to various users.

Highlight programs the library held : You Tube is medium for to share library activities or programme which library held. One can upload audiovisual clip of the programme on You Tube.

Advertise books, media, or other resources : Best books to read, my favorite book to read. We can advertise the book, or can promote to read. Our user community also can get inform on the particular best book, media or other e resources.

Encourage reading : Like that advertisement of books, we can encourage or inculcate the reading habits of the library community.

Advocate for libraries : Like this activity by librarian it advocate the library services and usefulness in our library society. Other user can attract toward the library and enhance the popularity of the library.

REACH SITE SUMMERY

Introduction

RSS stand for Reach Site Summery or Really Simple Syndication or RDF (Resource Description Framework) Site Summery. It is most popular and easy tool among Web 2.0 technologies. Basically RSS is a XML coding, with the help of that users can get websites updates in a personal manner without visiting the website. RSS is a defined standard based on XML with the specific purpose of delivering updates to web-based content. Using this standard, webmasters provide headlines and fresh content in a succinct manner. Meanwhile, consumers use RSS readers and news aggregators to collect and monitor their favorite feeds in one centralized program or location. Content viewed in the RSS reader or news aggregator is place known as an RSS feed.

RSS stands for Real Simple Syndication or Reach Site Summary. The technology, on one hand allows a web site to list the newest published updates (like table of contents of journals, new articles) through a technology called XML; on the other hand, it facilitates a web user to keep track new updates on chosen website(s). Like a personal search assistant, RSS feed readers visit predefined web sites, look for updated information and fetch it automatically on to the user's desktop. In order to use RSS Feed, users are required to download RSS feed reader and then subscribe to the RSS feeds from sites of their choice.

There are following two types of RSS feed reader:

- Stand-alone Desktop Reader (Mozilla / Free Reader 3.11, MS Office Outlook (2007 Version): These feed readers manage feed subscriptions and display subscribed content in a manner similar to most e-mail programs.
- Plug-in or Extension Desktop Reader or On Line Aggregators (for example RSS feeds toolbar for Microsoft Internet Explorer 1.2.0.1): The plug-in works with the user's web browser or e-mail client to display feeds available for viewing as a webpage and do not require additional software. The desktop readers and online aggregators offer a variety of features to help readers manage their feed subscriptions. Such features may include filtering feeds to highlight or delete

entries matching specific keywords combining several feeds into a single view and hiding entries that have already been viewed.

In the Use Study of Web 2.0 tools in World National Library (Webology Journal 2012), most of the national libraries are using it to communicate library's news and events. 36 percent national libraries are also using it as a blog feed. For example National Library of Canada, Trinidad and Tobago, USA, Maldives, Singapore, Ireland, UK, Australia and New Zealand are using on its blog so that user can easily get updates on the latest posting. Only six national libraries are using RSS to communicate recent changes in their collection. Use of RSS for providing updates on newsletters, podcast/vodcast and Flickr are quite less on the websites of national libraries. National Library of USA and Japan are making extensive use of RSS on their websites. On both the websites RSS feeds are properly categorized and each activity of libraries is connected with the RSS.

RSS History

RSS was first invented by Netscape. They wanted to use an XML format to distribute news, stories and information. Netscape refined the version of RSS and then dropped it. User Land Software to control of the specification and continued to develop it releasing a newer version. A noncommercial group picked up RSS at the same time and based on their interpretation of the Netscape's original concept of RSS they too released a new version. User Land was not happy with the noncommercial Version and continued development of their own version of RSS (Really Simple Syndication), eventually User Land released RSS. RSS feeds can be displayed – in a blog, on a website – and the user can grab your feed and display too

RSS Use in Library Services

RSS can be applied to some of the following Library and Information Services:

- Selective Dissemination of Information
- Current Awareness Service
- Bibliographic Service
- Bulletin Board Service
- RSS for Marketing Library & Information Services

Steps Involved in Using RSS Feeds

There are three steps involved in using RSS Feeds, i.e.

i. Download and install an RSS feed reader;

ii. Pick-up the RSS feeds from web sites of your interest;

iii. Add RSS feeds in the feed reader; and

iv. Click at RSS feeds added to the feed readers to get content from for feeds picked in step

Get RSS feed reader

This is the program that checks the websites for changes and updates. It will periodically scan those Sites and alert to what's new. Some readers are separate software applications that need Installation; others are Web-based programs, or perhaps are offered by major search sites such as Google and Yahoo There are a number of free RSS feed-reader programs available, and other programs that offer a free trial version. The following three RSS readers are free and run under

Windows

- SharpReader (www.sharpreader.com)
- RssReader (www.rssreader.com)
- FeedReader (www.feedreader.com)
- AmphetaDesk: (www.disobey.com/

Google (www.google.com/reader) and Yahoo! (http://my.yahoo.com), as well as many blogging services—like Bloglines (www.bloglines.com) and Newsgator (www.newsgator.com) offer RSS feed reading as part of their site's services. Download and install one of the RSS feed readers. Log on to the following URL to get a list of RSS feed readers that are available for free or on payment: http://www.dmoz.org/Computers/Software/Internet/Clients/WWW/Feed_Readers

Getting RSS Feeds

The second step is to pick-up RSS feeds from the web sites of your choice. RSS feeds are essentially URLs pointing to the updated information on a given topic on a site that a user can subscribe to. Cambridge University Press, for example, requires a user to register. Visit the CUP web site at http:// journals.cambridge.org/. Click at "Register Now" and follow the steps to get yourself registered. Once you are registered, you may require to "Log-in" for getting to the page where RSS Feeds are given. For logging-in to your account, type username and password in the "Log-in Form" then click on Login. Click on RSS /Atom feeds that appear under the browse menu in the left-hand navigation bar. User can also click on the RSS / Atom Icons that appear on individual journal homepage. It will take to the RSS/Atom feed page reproduced below:

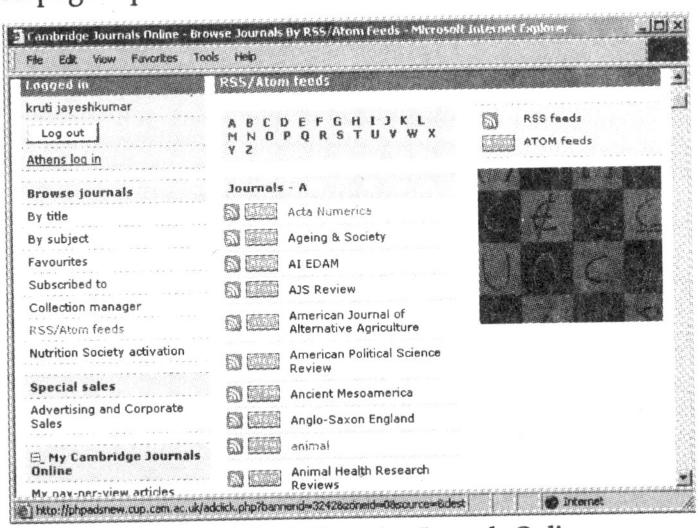

Fig. 26. RSS feeds Browsing Journals Online

Find the journal of your interest and click at the RSS icon next to it. This will open a new web page; at the bottom of the page, a user can see either one or two URLs. The first (or only) URL provides a feed for the latest issue of a particular journal. The feed contains a brief description of the journal along with list of the articles that appear in that issue. The second URL, if it is displayed, provides a feed for forthcoming articles. Select and copy these URLs

Add RSS Feeds in the Feed Reader

Open RSS Feed Reader and Click at "New" button to add RSS feeds to your feed reader. Paste the URL for RSS feed to the reader and click on OK button. A user is required to repeat this process for every feed, he / she wants to get feeds from

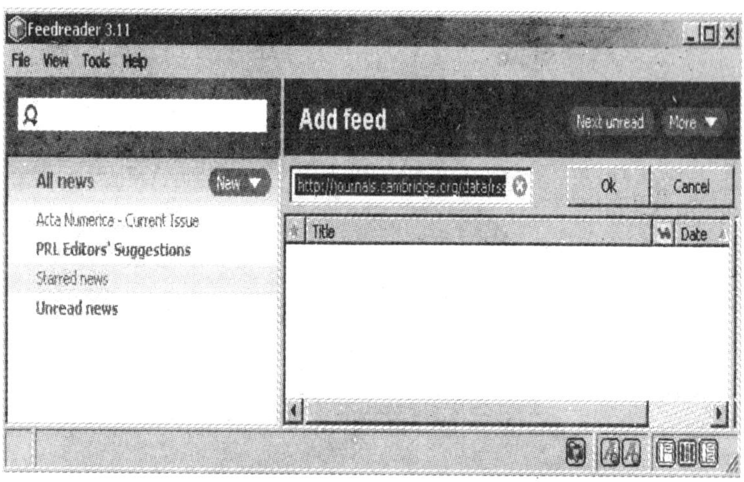

Fig. 27. RSS Feed Reader 3.11

Get Content for Selected Feeds

Click at the RSS feed (given in the left-hand side navigation bar) added to the RSS feed reader in the step given above.

The reader reads the contents

Once you've added the new feed address, your RSS feed reader will read the contents of the file. (In many readers, this is a temporary display and you will need to subscribe or execute another command that permanently adds the feed to your list.) The reader processes the file looking for changes since the last reading, then displays those changes

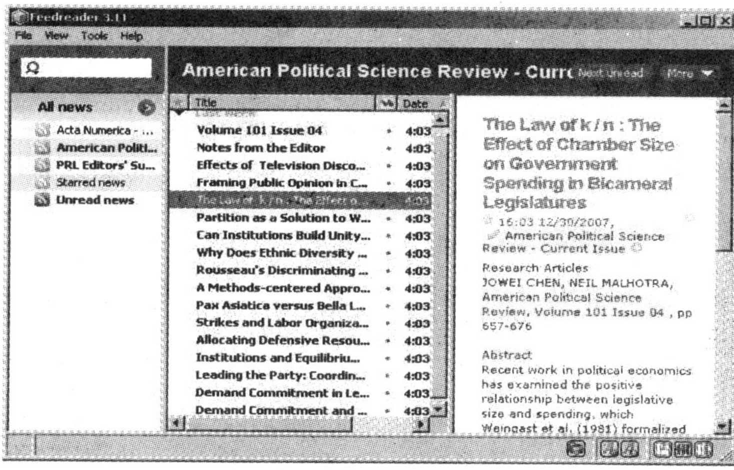

Fig. 28. Feed Reader getting Content.

Enjoy your feedback

From then on, whenever you open your reader or reader service, you will see the latest news from all your feeds. If you keep the reader running, it will continue to check your sites and alert you with an audio alarm and/or a pop-up when there is new information added. Once you've selected your preferred RSS reader and subscribed to a few feeds.

FLICKR

Flickr use for library marketing services and show the library working functions and hour also the flickr is tools to upload picture pictorial value of library. This can demonstrate Library collections, resources characteristics of the library. Library surroundings and environments to study in pictorial form, as following type of ideas are included in Flickr tools. As following Library of Congress pictorial web site on flickr shows that library locations and functions.

Fig. 21. The Library of Congress Flickr Home page

Free account or Pro account

It is perfectly feasible to sign up for the **free account** and use Flickr to organise your images without ever upgrading to a **Pro account**. If you are new to Flickr it's probably wise to start off with a free account before deciding whether it's going to be a useful tool. Yahoo owns Flickr, and in order to have any Flickr account (free or pro) you will first need to sign up for a free Yahoo ID. If you already have a Yahoo ID, you can use that on Flickr. The key benefits of the Pro account include **unlimited uploads, archiving of originals, unlimited sets** (albums for organizing your images), **ad-free browsing** and **access to statistics** about your images number of views, etc.

The main limitation of the free account is that you are restricted to uploading 100MB of photos per calendar month. Note that this is measured in bandwidth rather than actual space used – so if you upload 80MB of photos, you will only be able to upload another 20MB within the same month, even if you remove previously uploaded images It's worth pointing out here that the only image file formats you can upload are JPEGs, GIFs (non-animated) and PNGs. You can upload TIFFs but Flickr will convert them to JPEGs. It is also possible to upload some raw files, but they too will be converted to JPEGs and probably not in the way you would convert them yourself

Historic photography collections on Flickr

An increasing number of publicly-held photography collections are making selections of their images available through Flickr. Collections from around the world have contributed around 50,000 images so far, all of which have 'no known copyright restrictions' Photo from The Library of Congress on Flickr. This help increase awareness of and access to the photographs, it can help enrich the data held in the collections' catalogues by encouraging visitors to contribute any information they have about the photos via comments, notes and tags. The Library of Congress was the first to join The Commons and gave each image only one tag ('Library of Congress') - any other tags you see were added by the community; we are generally not controlling the content of Flickr tags, notes and comments. You can see how many tags have been added since the project was launched in January 2008.

After two years Library of Congress reported there had been over 23 million views of their 8,000 images and that *over a thousand records in the Prints and Photographs online catalogue have been enhanced with information from the Flickr Commons community.* Flickr is inviting other cultural heritage institutions to participate in The Commons.

Tags

Tags are extremely useful if you want to highlight aspects of the image that may not be covered by the description for example colors, time of day, weather, camera model, moods, concepts and so on. You can think of tags as keywords, which add a further dimension to an image's 'find ability'.

Some points you should consider when tagging :

- There is no 'controlled vocabulary' so tags are limited only by your imagination
- Tags can be single words, numbers or phrases
- There is no spellchecker
- There may be alternative ways of spelling the same thing (e.g. building names and place names)
- You may want to use more than one term to describe an object or concept
- Flickr is used globally, so you could think about using foreign languages and US spellings too.

Connecting Blog to Flickr

If you have a blog, it's very simple to set up a connection withFlickr. sAll the main blog services are supported, including Word **Press,** Blogger, **Typepad, LiveJournal, Movable Type** and **Twitter**. Once the connection is set up, you can post your Flickr images straight to your blog. You can also use this method to post images by other Flickr members on your blog when you see the 'Share this' button. Flickr also makes it easy to 'grab' the code to share or embed an image in any other website – some find this useful as they can keep all their images in one place and link to them from all their web presences main sites, blogs and other social networking sites such as Facebook.

Tags

Tags are extremely useful if you want to highlight

aspects of the image that may not be covered by the description – for example **colours, time of day, weather, camera model, moods, concepts** and so on. You can think of tags as keywords, which add a further dimension to an image's 'find ability'.

Some points you should consider when tagging:

- There is no 'controlled vocabulary' so tags are limited only by your imagination
- Tags can be single words, numbers or phrases
- There is no spellchecker (typos are rife on Flickr)
- There may be alternative ways of spelling the same thing (e.g. building names and place names)
- You may want to use more than one term to describe an object or concept
- Flickr is used globally, so you could think about using foreign languages and US spellings too
- You can let others add tags to your images (via the privacy and permissions settings

More ideas to use Flickr in Library:

Highlight library events : Flickr can highlight library current events. Librarian can upload recent snaps on the Library Flickr web. Therefore Flickr can highlight library events.

Hold a photo contest : we can hold photo contest on the flickr to do the get result of Flickr.

Upload a collection : Library can upload the all library collection of snaps to show library history in pictorial form.

Library tour : It is opportunity to display visual library visit or tour by uploading all library sections, services offered by photo or snap and way to access the physical library resources.

- Ask people to post pictures of themselves reading or using the library

- Create a sense of community

Available Feeds to use

- Public photos & video
- Friends' photostream
- Public favorites from a user
- Group discussions
- Group pools
- Forum discussions
- Recent activity on your photostream
- Recent comments you made

MASHUPS

Introduction

Mashups are perhaps the single conceptual foundation to all the technologies discussed in this article. They are apparently hybrid applications, where two or more technologies or services are conflated into a completely new, novel service. Retrieve, for example, conflates Flickr's image database and an experimental information architecture algorithm to enable users to search images not by metadata, but by the data itself. Users search for images by sketching images. In some ways, many of the technologies discussed above are mashups in their very nature. Another example is WikiBios, a site where users create online biographies of one another, essentially blending blogs with social networks. Library 2.0 is a mashup. It is a hybrid of blogs, wikis, streaming media, content aggregators, instant messaging, and social networks. Library 2.0 remembers a user when they log in. It allows the user to edit OPAC data and metadata, saves the user's tags, IM conversations with librarians, wiki entries with other users and catalogs all of these for others to use, and the user is able to make all or part of their profile public; users can see what other users have similar items checked-out, borrow and lend tags, and a giant user-driven catalog is created and mashed with the traditional catalog. Library 2.0 is completely user-centered and user-driven. It is a mashup of traditional library services and innovative Web 2.0 services. It is a library for the 21st century, rich in content, interactivity, and social activity. Combine data from multiple sources.

- Google Maps
- RSS feeds
- Catalogue

Functions Mashups

Data converters : language translators, speech processing, URL shorteners...

Communication : email, instant messaging, notification ...

Visual data rendering : information visualization, diagrams

Security related : electronic payment systems, ID identification...

LIBRARY THING

Library Thing is a social cataloging web application for storing and sharing book catalogs and various types of book metadata. It is used by individuals, authors, libraries and publishers. Based in Portland, Maine, Library Thing was developed by Tim Spalding and went live on August 29, 2005. As of April 2013 it has over 1,650,000 users and more than 80 million books catalogued. The primary feature of Library Thing is the cataloging of books by importing data from libraries through Z39.50 connections and from sixAmazon.com stores. Library sources supply MARC and Dublin Core records to LT; users can import information from 690 libraries, including the Library of Congress, National Library of Australia, the Canadian National

Catalogue, the British Library, and Yale University. Should a record not be available from any of these sources, it is also possible to add the book information by using a blank form.

Library Thing is majority owned by founder Tim Spalding. Online bookseller Abe Books (now owned by Amazon) bought a 40% share in LibraryThing in May 2006 for an undisclosed sum. In January 2009, Cambridge Information Group acquired a minority stake in the company, and their subsidiary Bowker became the official distributor to libraries.

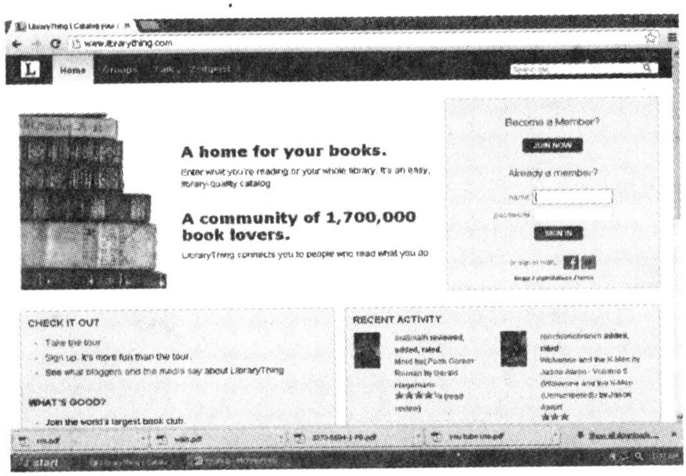

Fig. 30. Library Things Hompage.

3

Changing Skills and Competencies for Librarian 2.0

Skill is the unified force of experience intellect and passion in their operation. — **John Ruskin (1819-1900)**

INTRODUCTION

Library 2.0 Concept: According to Miller (2006) "Library 2.0" is a term coined by Michael Casey on his Library Crunch blogs. Though his writings on Library 2.0 are groundbreaking and in many ways authoritative, Casey (2006a) defines the term very broadly, arguing it applies beyond technological innovation and service. In addition to Casey, other blogging librarians have begun conceptually exploring what Library 2.0 might mean, and because of this disparate discussion with very wide parameters, there is some controversy over the definition and relative importance of the term. The nature of this controversy Lawson (2006), Peek (2005), and Tebbuti (2006) explore and begin to adequately rectify, and Crawford (2006) provides a very thorough account of the ambiguity and confusion surrounding the term, partially suggesting that there is nothing inherently novel about the idea.

The application of Library 2.0 theory to aspects of librarianship reaching beyond Web 2.0 technology is welcome, of course, but should very likely be framed by a different vocabulary. Indeed, Casey (2006a) recognizes the recurrence of similar ideas throughout library history, and Hale (1991) provides a landmark discussion of this user-centered philosophy external to web-services. There is simply no need to use the term "Library 2.0" in these environments. It is a much more useful theory if it is focused on web-services.

FEATURES OF LIBRARY 2.0

- It is user-centered. Users participate in the creation of the content and services they view within the library's web-presence, OPAC, etc. The consumption and creation of content is dynamic, and thus the roles of librarian and user are not always clear.
- It provides a multi-media experience. Both the collections and services of Library 2.0 contain video and audio components. While this is not often cited as a function of Library 2.0, it is here suggested that it should be.
- It is socially rich. The library's web-presence includes users' presences. There are both synchronous (e.g. IM) and asynchronous (e.g. wikis) ways for users to communicate with one another and with librarians.
- It is communally innovative. This is perhaps the single most important aspect of Library 2.0. It rests on the foundation of libraries as a community service, but understands that as communities change, libraries

must not only change with them, and they must allow users to change the library. It seeks to continually change its services, to find new ways to allow communities, not just individuals to seek, find, and utilize information.

APPLICATION OF WEB 2.0 TOOLS IN LIBRARY

Library Blogs : Blogs is a website, usually maintained by an individual, contains chronologically the brief entries of commentary, description of events, or other material like audio video, graphics. Etc. Promoting library's services, resources, and programmes online become a lot of easier with the help of a blog. Library blog's can be very effective tools for reaching online.

1. Marketing of library services
2. Promoting Library Services
3. Supporting Users
4. Community Engagements
5. Other Application of Blogs in Libraries:
6. Current Awareness Service
7. Selective Dissemination of Inforamtion
8. To highlight news or resources of interest
9. To post book reviews from student, faculty and staff members
10. To announce new acquisition in Library
11. To use as Library newsletter
12. To use as reference desk
13. To use as Libraries consortia

To Link recommended web sites. as a "first of the social software" Giustini, 2006) which is also described as "chronological social web site" (Blog 2008). Blogs have become a very popular, easy and social platform to exchange information, and gradually are becoming a more acceptable reference sources even in peer reviewed publications. Service can be providing effectively through the blogs.

In this connection, specialization of the blogs plays a crucial role in timeliness, perfection, and accuracy of blogs. Specialization saves the time of the users while searching through massive amount of uncontrolled information if every field is mixed up. Specialization is a best way to optimize the potential use of blogs if they are provided through non-conventional library services and information delivery

WIKIS : Is the other popular tool of Web 2.0, which is a suitable platform for reference and information services in Library and information centers. The collaborative nature of wikis provides opportunity for instantaneous revision as well as to develop an efficient repository of new information. In sciences, case studies as a source of evidence play a vital role while they are not categorized in formal sources of information like books, thesis, journal, etc. hence most of the time they are being left without being organized. The only chance for utilizing case studies is when they are reported through a journal. Wiki can be used as an open-source depository of case studies and finally a best source of evidences.

Slide Shares, Video Shares and Photo Shares : are appropriate community tools to share medical images, atlases, educational video clips in medical libraries. They can be created and shared by consumers as well as professionals. Librarians can digitalize the images embedded in atlases and books to share the pictures with educational purposes such as

Podcasts : as one of the facets of Web 2.0 have great impacts in education. Nowadays, podcasts are being used in patient education. USA education system values the podcast method in the educational process. Several American universities, including Drexel and Duke, have recently distributed iPods to their students, and have experimented with podcasting. Presently, several organizational Web sites are using podcasts. It can use for music library.

Really Simple Syndication (RSS) : gives the possibility of being informed about new items added to the interested site. Librarians can utilize the RSS feeds to catch up trends and changes of desired specialty, and simultaneously to give the same opportunity to user community to keep themselves up-to-date. RSS feeds act as the neo-conventional library services of sending alert to users about new items added to the library holding, or sending table of contents of interested journals to specific users. In a way it serves as an effective SDI services.

Perpetual searching for the specific information and given source for information is always tiresome for professionals/individuals as well as librarians when they want to send SDI services to their user. RSS feed is a social tool that ensures easy, fast and certain accessibility of specific up-to-date information.

Furthermore, not only Web 2.0 applications are useful in information services but they are also applicable in organization of information through tools like folksonomy.

Folksonomy : among all the tools of Web 2.0, the more debatable one in the library science area is the folksonomy. It is for several decades that library science advocates use of controlled vocabulary, thesaurus, and taxonomy and authority control in classifying, storing and retrieving information on the Web. User constructed tag or folksonomy is something different even more arbitrary than natural language. Since users may use slangs, inefficient and incomplete words and sometime irrelevant words for tagging the created documents, which causes irrelevant and misleading information retrieval. But it is a very appropriate way to carry out user studies to find out the preferences of the users in information searching as well as information tagging. The study of user behavior in using key words in their queries will enable librarians/ information specialists to organize the information efficiently and support the search engines, indexing tools, folksonomy-based systems like Delicious on the Web and digital era in an appropriate way based on the users' preferences and approaches.

Web Opac : Web OPAC online public Access Catalogue is a web based search platform, developed with advance information technology technologies for serving information to the users at the fingerprints, regardless of physical location whether the number is in the library or at a remote location. It brings the library online by presenting bibliographic data in a read-only manner. Following are some of the library services which can be made available through web OPAC.

1. Library Catalogue
2. Search facility on entire database
3. New arrivals, current Awareness Services
4. Selective Dissemination of information
5. Journal List
6. Online Journal
7. Latest issues of Journals
8. Popular Documents based on circulation and reservation
9. Place Reservation/ hold on certain documents
10. Outstanding list- renewal facility optional
11. Procurements request for purchasing new books and other media
12. Approve documents for procurements
13. User feedback

Librarian 2.0 : Librarian 2.0 understands end users

deeply in terms of their goals and aspirations, workflows, social and content needs, and more. Librarian 2.0 is where the user is, when the user is there. This is an immersion environment that librarians are eminently qualified to contribute to, Aspects of librarian influenced e-learning and distance education as implemented by our institutions and communities should allow us to contribute to the preparation of our users to acquire and improve their skills and competencies. It is essential that we start preparing to become Librarian 2.0 now. The Web 2.0 movement is laying the groundwork for exponential business growth and another major shift in the way our users live, work, and play. We have the ability, insight, and knowledge to influence the creation of this new dynamic

Librarian 2.0 Objective

- Understand the power of the Web 2.0 opportunities
- Learn the major tools of Web 2.0 and Library 2.0 Blog, Wikis,
- Combine e-resources and print formats and is container and format agnostic
- Is device independent and uses and delivers to everything from laptops

To PDAs to iPods

- Develop targeted federated search and adopts the Open URL standard
- Connect people and technology and information in context
- doesn't shy away from non-traditional cataloging and classification and chooses tagging, tag clouds, folksonomies, and user-driven content descriptions and classifications where appropriate
- Embrace non-textual information and the power of pictures, moving images, sight, and sound

- understand the "long tail" and leverages the power of old and new content
- See the potential in using content sources like the Open Content Alliance, Google Print, and Open WorldCat
- Connect users to expert discussions, conversations, and communities of practice and participates there as well
- Use the latest tools of communication (such as Skype) to connect content, expertise, information coaching, and people.
- Use and develops advanced social networks to enterprise advantage
- Connect with everyone using their communication mode of choice – telephone, Skype, IM, SMS, texting, email, virtual reference, etc
- Encourage user driven metadata and user developed content and commentary
- Understand the wisdom of crowds and the emerging roles and impacts of the blogosphere, Web syndicasphere and wikisphere first and foremost; Librarian 2.0 understands his or her users at a deep level.

Librarian 2.0: Competencies and Skills

For Librarian 2.0 some competencies and skills required for to satisfy user need through web based library environments it is as following.

David's Library 2.0 Competencies: David leeking has given some competencies for Librarian 2.0 as following.

- write and post to a blog
- add photos and videos to a blog post
- embed a widget into blogs and social networking accounts (like Myspace)
- social network knowledge – basic understanding of

Facebook, Myspace, Twitter, etc

- shoot, upload and edit photos
- shoot, upload and edit short videos
- record, edit and upload a podcast
- use IM in different forms
- use and explain rss and rss readers to others
- send and read sms text messages
- edit an avatar's appearance
- basic console gaming skills (multiple formats preferred

Skills

Librarians 2.0 plans for their users : This librarian bases all planning and proposals for services, materials and outreach on user needs and wants. User-centered libraries breakdown barriers and allow users access wherever they are: home, work, commuting, school, or at the library. This involves users from the get go in planning and launching services based on their needs. This librarian asks what new technologies or new materials users need. This librarian proposes building projects and involves users in designing those places. This librarian does not create policies and procedures that impede users' access to the library. This librarian tells users how resources and funds will be expended. Decisions and plans are discussed in open forums and comments are answered. This makes the library transparent.

Librarian 2.0 embraces Web 2.0 tools : This librarian recognizes how services might be enhanced by the Read/ Write web and how new services might be born in a climate of collaboration. This librarian uses Instant Messaging to meet users in their space online, builds Weblogs and wikis as resources to further the mission of the library, and mashes up content via API (Application Program Interface) to build useful Web sites. A Google map mash up of local libraries created by Chicago librarians is one such instance of building tools via new resources. Other librarians creating My Space profiles and participating in other thriving communities build connections online where their users live.

Librarian 2.0 controls techno lust : This librarian does not buy technology for the sake of technology. "Techno-worship" does not exist here. Without a firm foundation in the mission and goals of the institution, new technologies are not implemented for the sake of coolness and status. Technology is put to the test: Does it meet the users need in a new or improved way? Does it create a useful service for putting users together with the information and experience they seek? These are some of the questions this librarian asks when planning for technology. This librarian creates and nurtures a living, breathing technology plan.

Librarian 2.0 makes good, yet fast decisions : This librarian recognizes how quickly the world and library users change with advancing technology. Project timelines that stretch on for months simply do not work in Library 2.0 thinking. Perpetual beta works well for the library's Web presence. This librarian redesigns for ease of use, user involvement and easily added/re-configured pieces. This librarian brings evidence to the table for planning sessions and decision making.

Librarian 2.0 is a trends potter : This librarian seeks out information and news that may impact future services. This librarian uses human conversations need to take place within their institution, virtually and in physical space. This librarian reads outside the profession and watches for the impact of technology on users and new thinking on business, because it is, in fact, related.

Librarian 2.0 gets content : This librarian understands that the future of libraries will be guided by how users access, consume and create content. Content is a conversation as well and librarians should participate. Users will create their own mashups, remixes and original expressions and should be able to do so at the library or via the library's resources. This librarian will help users become their own programming director for all of the content available to them. Librarian 2.0 also listens to staff and users when planning, tells the stories of successes and failures, learns from both, celebrates those successes, allows staff time to play and learn, and never stops dreaming about the best library services

CONCLUSION

Library 2.0 is a user-centered virtual community. It is a socially rich, often egalitarian electronic space. While Librarian 2.0 might act as a facilitator and provide support, he or she is not necessarily primarily responsible for the creation of the content. Users interact with and create resources with one another and with librarians. In some ways, it is a virtual reality for libraries, a Web manifestation of the library as place. A library's presence on the Web in Library 2.0 includes the presence of that library's constituency and utilizes the same applications and technologies as its community.

SKILLS AND COMPETANCY FOR LIS PROFESSIONAL IN ICT ERA

a. Information Technology

Information technology has defined as follows Definition: Macmillan Dictionary defines information technology as acquisition, processing storage and dissemination of vocal, verbal, pictorial, textual and numerical information by microelectronic based combination of computer and telecommunication.

UNESCO has defined "information technology the scientific, technological and engineering discipline and the management techniques used in information handling and processing, their application, computer and their interaction with men and machine, and associated social, economic and cultural matters"

According to ALA Glossary, "Information technology is the application of computer storage retrieval and dissemination of information. In fact fusion of information science and technology has given birth to a new discipline called information technology"

Webstars New Encyclopedia of information technology is "the collective term for the various technologies involved in the processing and transmission of information. They include computing, telecommunication and microelectronics".

We may reveal from the above definition that information technology is a combination of various technologies such as computer technology, telecommunication system and such as computer technology, telecommunication system and services, micrographic and reprographic technologies and information storage technology. Thus we can define information technology as those processes and technologies which are used acquisition and dissemination of information based on electronic technology.

Component of Information Technology: Information technology developed throughout the ages, but there was always a change in the materials and techniques used for recording, storage, processing and combination of information. Following are the major components

b. Computer Technology

The computer is most useful modern tool yet developed. Today we are using computer in ever increasing numbers. In way never imagined just a few years ago. The computer is an electronic tool which works with high speed, accuracy, and memory. It stores processes and retrieves information in a very efficient way.

c. Communication Technology

Communication is the process of transmitting information. Without proper communication of information cannot reach its defined destination. The technology used in transmitting information is called communication technology. The communication technology comes in picture if the range of communication is such that direct communication system must be used.

d. Multimedia Technology

The term Multimedia refers to delivering information in a simpler and easy way to end users using text, pictures and images. It is widely used and simply presents the information in text, graphics, images video, audio and animation interactively environment. Multimedia information kiosk is one of the most important application libraries.

e. CD Rom Technology

ROM is abbreviation of compact Disk read only memory, and is a optical disk which has the capacity of holding information equivalent to 1000 double side double density floppies. It is a silver plated disk must be passed through a player of the disk. Unlike floppy disks, CD ROM's are passed from a master copy instead of being recorded one by one. This optical disk capacity is 60 megabits. The important characteristic of it is that it can be stored data equivalent to 1500 floppy disks. Database technology: Database can be defined as a collection of interrelated data stored so that it may be accessed by authorized users with simpler user friendly dialogues. Sharing of information through e-mails, FTP, TELNET, GOPHER, Online facilities or terminal is possible if a data base is present.

f. Networking Technology

Networking is means through, which two computers can talk to each other so many networks operational throughout the world. As NICNET, INDONET, ERNET, NISSAT, CALIBNET, BONET, DELNET, MALIBNET, BALNET.

g. Barcode Technology

Barcode can be defined as a self contained message with information encoded in a series of black bars of varying breadths and white spaces between every two of them, the bars and space between every two of them. The bars and spaces represent a series of characteristic or digits. These are readable only by a scanner which sends messages to the computer that deco defy the number of the digits. The computer identifies such bars as 0s and 1s (zeros and ones) white blanks as off's and one's.

h. Digital Technology

The use of digital technology has paved the way of emerging digital as well as virtual libraries. The term digital library may be understood in different way and named differently. In Digital libraries, services are fully automated and all resources are in digital form and they are heterogeneous in nature. These include work related to information and how to digitize, store, find, link, visualize, use, publish, manage and share information.

i. Virtual Reality

Virtual Library is library without resource but resources simply may be a collection of web sources. It is the library with little or no physical presence of books, periodicals, readings space or support staff, but is the one that disseminates information directly to the distributed users, usually electronically. The virtual library is the output of virtual reality, which is a substitution of manmade input to one or more of the senses. Thus virtual reality is a technology that provide with sensation and the control of perspective so that provide with sensations and the control of perspective so that one experiences the illusion of being in the presence of the object within a situation

Policy Initiatives for ICT in Higher Education

Snehi Neeru, (2009) stated in his article ICT in Indian Universities and Colleges: Opportunities and challenges that Indian policy for developing ICTs as a vehicle for promoting education is visible since the use of satellite in early 1970s, launching of dedicated satellite for education (EDUSAT). In addition the National Task Force on Information Technology and Software Development: IT Action Plan Part III- Long Term National IT Policy (GOI, 1999) constituted by the then Prime Minister of India in 1998 gave fillip to efforts for exploiting rapidly emerging new technologies. Major emphasis of the Policy was on expansion of IT education at school and university level including all national level institutions.

Higher education

18064 colleges/institutions

378 universities

Promotion of use and integration of ICTs in education would immensely benefit the socio-economic development of the country (11th FYP). Meanwhile, the Tenth Plan provided the necessary driving force for use of ICTs in higher education in the twenty first century. Subsequently, the UGC initiated scheme called "ICT for teaching and learning process" for achieving quality and excellence in higher education. Network facilities with the help of ERNET, Ministry of Information and Technology, Government of India were installed at UGC office to promote a healthy work culture. Along with this UGC launched a mega programme namely, 'UGC INFONET', a network of Indian Universities and Colleges, by integrating Information and Communication Technology (ICT) in the process of teaching, learning and education management. The network is managed by ERNET India and almost all the universities are its members. Information for Library Network (INFLIBNET), an autonomous Inter University Centre of UGC is the nodal agency for coordination and facilitation of the linkage between ERNET and Universities. In addition, UGC is encouraging creation of e-content / learning material for teaching learning process and management of education in colleges and universities. UGC is also collaborating with other organizations like Intel by signing MOUs to integrate and introduce ICTs effectively in higher education institutions. These initiatives have received recognition as well as push in the Eleventh Five Year Plan. The significant impact of ICTs in the delivery of educational services has led to allocation of large amount i.e. Rs.5000 crores for providing ICT infrastructure in government and government –aided secondary and senior secondary schools during the Eleventh Plan period. In higher education sector also, a National Mission in Education through ICTs is planned to be launched to increase ICT coverage in all the 378 universities and 18064 colleges. The Mission will focus on digitization and networking of all educational institutions, developing low cost and low power consuming access devices, and making available bandwidth for educational purposes. These initiatives would provide significant opportunities and pose new challenges as well for effective use of ICT in programme delivery (11th FYP). Nevertheless, introduction of ICTs in the higher education has profound implications for the whole education process ranging from investment to use of technologies in dealing with key issues of access, equity, management, efficiency, pedagogy, quality, research and innovation. Therefore, the next section attempts to delineate the role of ICTs in higher education sector.

ROLE OF ICT IN HIGHER EDUCATION

Swift growth of ICTs is taking place all over the world. They have emerged as powerful tools for diffusion of knowledge and information. Their introduction and unprecedented use in the higher education has generated varied response. On the one hand there is acceptance of its potential benefits to knowledge creation i.e. field of research and its dissemination and on the other extreme it is feared that there use will further the digital divide/ inequity. It is inevitable that their increasing use in education system will also raise issues regarding what kind of technologies, in what quantity, at what level and for what purpose they need to be introduced. Nevertheless, the opportunities and challenges raised at different platforms can be categorized as the aspects relating to role of ICT for access and equity in education, role in management and efficiency in education, their role in pedagogy for quality learning and teaching at higher education level and in inducing innovations in approaches.

Developing E-Content

Locally relevant and learner centered e-content/ applications are a priority. This has implications for generating capacity to facilitate institutions/ industry for e-content development and its marketing. The best practices incretion of e-content, its dissemination, criteria for selection and evaluation requires large scale networking among e-content users and producers. Issues pertaining to intellectual property rights in this multi-stakeholder activity are a major concern

National Knowledge Commission of India

This need librarian to update or to survive, establish a knowledge-oriented paradigm of development and to address the digital divide in India, the Government of India has established National Knowledge Commission in June 2005 with the following Terms of Reference

- Build excellence in the educational system to meet the knowledge challenges of the 21st century and increase India's competitive advantage in fields of knowledge.
- Promote creation of knowledge in S&T laboratories.
- Improve the management of institutions engaged in intellectual property rights.
- Promote knowledge applications in agriculture and industry.

Promote the use of knowledge capabilities in making government an effective, transparent and accountable service provider to the citizen and promote widespread sharing of knowledge to maximize public benefit. The National Knowledge Commission (NKC) has five distinct focus areas:

(i) Access to Knowledge : Providing access to knowledge resources through strengthening library and information infrastructure and networks, promoting and adopting open access literature, open courseware and open source software.

(ii) Knowledge Concepts : Nurturing intellectual capabilities and enhancing professional skills, including information handling skills of youths

(iii) Knowledge Creation : Making self-sufficiency in knowledge creation; strengthening indigenous research capabilities in science, technology and medicine (STM) areas; generating knowledge for social development.

(iv) Knowledge Application : Deriving maximum benefits from intellectual assets, applying knowledge in fields like agriculture, industry, health, education, etc. where productivity can be enhanced.

(v) Knowledge Services : Making governance and government functionaries more accountable, transparent, efficient and sensitive to the causes of common men. Indicates that how information literacy of stakeholders can enhance the capabilities of a nation for optimum utilization of knowledge resources. Information literacy can also make creation and generation of new knowledge a reality.

5. The Librarian's skill

Dr. Ranganathan's law "every book its reader" is like librarian has acted as the intermediary between the reader and the book. Only occasionally an interpreter, this was largely a passive role and tasks would be centered on the materials: selection, acquisition, purchasing organizing, storage, displaying, protecting, and evaluating improving work of the librarian. Now and in the coming decades the librarian's skill's has become much more diverse.

The librarian continues to acquire resources in many formats and media, local and remote for use in library or online; maybe acquisition is contracted out selects resources; a mix of research and evaluation, matching resources to changing audiences of actual and potential users; responding to community profiling, as in marketing; sometimes devising a brief to outsource works closely in partnership on joint projects according to a plan or strategy that is evaluated for outcomes and impact reaches outwards to inform, attract and respond to users. At the same time – public, college, university, health, special library... different libraries provide for different needs, at different stages of learning but on a continuum – early years, family learning, school, studying the academic library – students, learners, researchers, academics, entrepreneurs and academic partner organizations, corporate and industry bodies, local, regional and national Government researches innovation or tests products and services with users evaluates through user survey and user-benefit analysis or cost-benefit analysis (John Dolan OBE, 2009) Therefore to fulfill library objectives LIS professional needs to update himself with technology

5.1. Librarians Soft skill

Soft skill is essentially people skill the non technical, personality specific skill that determines your strengths as a leader, listener, negotiator, and conflict mediator. Following skills and soft skill required for library professional

BODY LANGUAGE

It is Non-verbal language Face is the index of the mind and it clearly displays the person's interest Body language presents to the audience what we feel & think about the particular matter Ex: Nodding one's head Body language (e.g., arms crossed, standing, sitting, relaxed) Emotion of the sender & receiver (e.g., speaking clearly, enthusiastic)

Written communication skill

Writing evaluates a person's proficiency indications, spelling grammar etc... Errors committed while writing circulars, reports & agenda considerably spoil the image of the writer Good visual presentation using graphics, color, and balanced design layout- adds so much to written communication. Keep handouts and other written materials for your presentation.

Presentation Skills

Presentation skills include planning, preparation & delivery of the message making a formal speech is one form of presentation. Presentation skills can be broadly categorized into physical oral, & electronic. Success in life depends on presenting ideas in an appropriate manners Look at the eyes of audience & speak in a natural, conversational voice Appropriate voice will make the presentation effective and interesting Ask for feedback from your audience about your presentation & change accordingly In presentation especially, stop occasionally to ask the audience understand what you have said

Team Work

People of gender, different age groups, qualification,

status & skills work as a team with a common objective of accomplishing the task the success of any organization largely depends on in the coordinated efforts of its employees It mainly refers to the agreeableness & co-operation among the team members

Professional ethics

Professional ethics is the need of the hour in India When a person is at the work spot, he must think of his work only He must put his heart & soul into the work each employee is a organic part of the organization & must strive to contribute his mite to the successful functioning of the organization

Interpersonal Skills

Man is a social animal & his success in life largely depends on his relationship & interaction with others we must respect the views & sentiments of others. When we desire to differ their views, we must very politely give hints to them without wondering their feelings

Time & Stress Management

Prioritize the work & schedule your time accordingly Impotent work should be allotted more time & taken up first Listening to classical music & practicing Yoga will considerably reduce the physical, emotional & mental stress of an individual

Leadership Communication Skills

Leaders, executives & managers need to be very clear about what they expect from others Trust yourself, Keep smiling, Share & stay together, Always learn new things, Accept responsibility for yourself & your actions ,Look at problems & challenges, Be grateful always, Love your self

Required ICT Skills and Competency

Information and communication Technology era LIS professional required Competencies needed as following:

Traditional Skills

It includes like cataloguing, acquisitions, reference and information search skills

Value-Adding Skills

Including research skills and skills in synthesizing and packaging information to support clients' work and decision-making

Soft Skills

That is generic and cut across disciplines, especially skills in communication, management, leadership, teaching and training, and teamwork, as well as the ability to empathize with users and understand their information needs

Appropriate Attitudes, Values and Personal Traits, especially those of user orientation and service orientation, flexibility and willingness to handle a wide range of tasks, adaptability and ability to handle change, continual learning, and an entrepreneurial attitude

Domain Knowledge (subject knowledge) that is specific to the type of information service or organization they are working in. Traditional skills are still in demand, but they have to be expanded to handle new digital formats and the online (especially Internet) environment. (Christopher Soo-Guan Khoo, 2005)

Traditional LIS skills extended to the handling of digital and online resources, including acquisition, cataloguing and organization of resources, metadata schemes, reference/information services, information packaging, circulation, preservation, online reference service,

Information search skills, copyright and intellectual property laws, user behavior, user needs, information sources, packaging of information, management of digital and hybrid libraries, evaluation of information and information sources, knowledge of information flows in society

Information management, including information audit, knowledge management

IT skills, including Internet, Web and XML technologies, RFID, federated search Engines, programming and scripting, Windows operating system, productivity tools (e.g. word processing, spreadsheet, database, planning tools, etc)

Transferable/generic skills applied to the library environment, including communication, public speaking, writing, public relations, interpersonal/group skills, networking, research skills, interviewing and listening skills, conducting focus groups, analytical skills, teamwork, multi-tasking, time management

Teaching, training and coaching, including skills for providing user education and training in an E-learning environment, developing e-learning and computer-based learning materials, facilitating collaborative learning

Management and leadership, including planning, financial management, budgeting, project management, negotiation and persuasion, supervisory skills, performance management/evaluation, administrative skills, human resource, outsourcing, quality management, ability to motivate subordinates, lead groups effectively, strategic planning Entrepreneurship, including business analysis and market research, marketing, fee-based information service, networking skills across job functions and levels

Attitudes and professional values, including user-orientation, service-orientation, belief in the pursuit of knowledge, love of learning, ability to read and respond to novel situations, intellectual curiosity, interaction with members of the profession, ability to articulate the roles of libraries and librarians

Other skills/knowledge: operation of call centers,

publishing, Internet publishing **(Christopher Soo-Guan Khoo, 2005)**

KNOWLEDGE MANAGEMENT WITH LIBRARY 2.0 TOOLS

The human has entered in a new phase of its evaluation, particularly with inception of the 21st century. It holds the prospectus of intellectual, material, technological and spiritual dimension of life. We experiencing this century as a knowledge age. With continues research and development and flow of knowledge has increased. In this knowledge age, society demands fast and updated knowledge for further development. Library is a heart of knowledge society for to satisfy knowledge demands and needs Libraries tries to change itself to connect its user by user known web technology. Today web technology is a tools of interaction, collaboration of content, sharing a views and ideas, collection of semantic resources, preservation of archival and dissemination to worldwide. So, this web technology applied in Library for knowledge management.

Definition

Knowledge Management : Management of activities and processes aimed at increasing the use and creation of knowledge on an organization with two complementary aims: a "patrimonial" objective and a durable innovation objective; these objectives are underlined by their economic, strategic, organizational, socio-cultural, and technological dimensions (Grundstein, 2004).Based on definitions of Grundstein (2004) and O'Leary (1998), we define knowledge management (KM) as the "Management of knowledge resources of an organization in order to ease: access, sharing, reuse of this knowledge (that can be explicit or tacit, individual or collective), with an objective of capitalization; Creation of new knowledge, with an objective of innovation."

Above definition states following types of flow of knowledge

- Knowledge creation, discovery, capture
- Knowledge storage, retention, organization
- Knowledge transfer, sharing, distribution
- Knowledge use & maintenance
- Knowledge management and library 2.0 tools: discussion

With wide range of information explosions and heterogeneous need of the Knowledge, Library professionals need to manage knowledge. They should use user interested technology and user friendly techniques to access free flow of information and knowledge. With continues innovation in web by Tim Berners-Lee creating more semantic web or user friendly web. Web 2.0 is a set of Web based software service that encourage user to become more involved in the creation and manipulation of data. Key technology used for web 2.0 is AJAX, blogs, RSS, WIKIS and XML. Advancement in web 2.0 facilitate user to access information and share their views with area of interested community. Web 2.0 helps in creation, discovery, storage, organization, transfer, distribution and use of knowledge. It means a great interaction and knowledge use by Web 2.0 environment. A library professional has applied this to create ideas to interact with community. And share their views and store and disseminate knowledge through Library Blogs, Wikis, Slide share, video share, RSS, Folksonomy, Podcasting, WebOPAC etc. which is user-centered, provides a multi-media experience, also socially rich, and also it is communally innovative.

REFERENCES

1. Bradley Phil (2007) How to use web 2.0 in your library London facet publishing, p. 38.

2. Bradley, P. (2007). How to use Web http://www.inflibnet.ac.in/UGC-InfoNet/ugcinfonet.html#5).

3. Brown Elizabeth, Maximiek Sarah, and Erin E. Rushton (2008) Connecting to Students: Launching Instant Messaging Reference at Binghamton University

4. Barsky E., & Purdon, M. (2006). Introducing web 2.0: social networking and social bookmarking for health libraries.*JCHLA/JABBS*, 27, 65-67.

5. Breeding marshall (2007) we need to go beyond web 2.0 computers n libraries 27 22-26

6. Casey, M. (2006b). LibraryCrunch: bringing you a library 2.0 perspective. Accessed May 18, 2006, from http://www.librarycrunch.com,

7. Dixon Angela (2012) Social Bookmarking, SVEA Training Modules Germany

8. Foley Marianne (Jan 2002) Instant Messaging Reference in an Academic Library- : a case study.

9. Gabriela Grosseck, Carmen Holotescu, (2008) Can we use twitter for educational activities, Forth International Conference e-learning and software for Education Bucharist.

10. Jadon N.s. Jadon Gopal singh and Rajput prabhat singh (2007), Library 2.0 and web 2.0 emerging technologies: its application in libraries. In developing library and information resources and services in the internet era, 53 rd all India library conference proceeding, hydrabad, December 13-14 2007 pp 266-272.

11. Jagdish Arora, Ashok Kumar,(2010) User Guide and Tutorials on E-resources p n.12-14

12. Jane Secker (2008) Libraries and Face book, London School of Economics and Political Science, Funded by: University of London Centre for Distance Education Teaching and Research Awards.

13. Kaushik Anna (2010 June) podcasting in library environment, annuls of library and information studies. p.p. 122

14. Miller, paul (2005) web 2.0: building the new library, ariadne, 45 (retrived December 28 2012 from http: //www.aradne.ac.uk/issue 45/miller.

15. Michelle McLean (2008) Web 2.0 and Libraries Innov8: Business solution for the next Wave.

16. Library 2.0 Theory: Web 2.0 and Its Implications for Libraries / http://www.webology.org/2006

17. Nabin Chandra Dey Pronab Sarkar, (2007) RSS Feeds and its Application in Library Services: 7th International CALIBER-2009, Pondicherry University, Puduchery, February 25-27, 2009 p. no 342-347

18. O'Reilly, T. (2005). *What is Web 2.0: design patterns and business models for the next generation of software*? Retrieved November 11, 2012, from http://oreilly.com/web2/archive/what-is-web-20.html

19. Ohdedar, A. K. *The Growth of the Library in ModernIndia: 1498-1836*. Calcutta: The World Press Private Limited, 1969. p.159.

20. Ranganathan S.R. School and college Libraries: madras Library Association, madras, 1942

21. Redman L.V. and A.V.H. Mory, the Romance of Research, 1923, p.10.

22. Remmic Incelory : College Handbook on Library Practice College Librarianship New delhi 1989 p.99

23. Ruth J.T. Edi.: the management it's selection of reading for libraries; 1986 p.20

24. **Snehi Neeru, (2009)** ICT in Indian Universities and Colleges: Opportunities and challenges: IILM Institute for Higher Education Management & Change, Volume 13, and Number 2.

25. **Sarah Milstein (sarah.milstein@gmail.com; http://twitter.com/sarahm) is** a co-author of "Twitter and the Micromessaging Revolution," a research report from O'Reilly Media. Her webcast on "Twitter for Business" is available at O'Reilly TV on YouTube **(www.youtube.com/watch?v=lUR2E8l3bi8)**.

26. Manorama Tripathi, Sunil Kumar (2010) Use of Web 2.0 tools in academic libraries: a reconnaissance of the international landscape, the International Information & Library Review.

27. Matthew M. Bejune (2007) Wikis in Libraries information technology and libraries

28. Ramesh Babu b. Narendra Kumar, A M. and Rao P Nageswara (2010) recent Developments in web 2.0: New avenues for LIS Professionals. Inforamtion age, 4, 3: 5-10.

29. Spivack, Nova (2006) the third generation web is coming www.kurzweilal.net on date 20th 7 2013

30. Tebbutt, D. (2006). Is all the talk of web 2.0 just a lot of codswallop? *Information World Review*, (221), 9-9.

31. Thanuskodi S. (2011) WEB 2.0 Awareness among Library and Information Science Professionals of the Engineering Colleges in

Chennai City: A Survey J Communication, 1(2): 69-75

Web

1. *http://www.en.Wikipedia/wiki/.college_library)*
2. *http://orangecopper.com/blog/list-of the -best social networking websites-2011 (retrived on June 2013-07-21*
3. **http://www.oreillynet.com/pub/a/oreilly/tim/news/2005/09/30/what-is-web-20.html**
4. http://www.brandwatch.com/2011/09/10-of-the-weirdest-social-networks/
5. http://digg.com/ on date 30/7/2013
6. http://www.podomatic.com/directory download on date 26/9/2013
7. http://www.vaidyanathcollegelibrary.blogspot.com
8. http://www.businessproductivity.com/does-instant-messaging-in-the-workplace-increase-business-productivity 26/7/2013
9. http://www.pingspider.com/socialbookmarking/the-history-of-social-bookmarking/ download on 29/7/2013
10. http://en.wikipedia.org/wiki/Social_bookmarking 26/9/2013
11. http: //www. libsuccess.org
12. http://twitter.com/NPR
13. http://twitter.com/BL_Ref_Service
14. www.youtube.com/watch?v=lUR2E8l3bi8
15. http://twitter.com/sarahm
16. http://twitter.com/jstor
17. http://www.wikipedia.org/wiki/main.page
18. http://www.delcious.com
19. http://www.simpy.co/
20. http:// www.connotea.org
21. http://citeulike.org,
22. Citeulike is a free service for managing and discovering scholarly references
23. http://www.diigo.com
24. http://www.digg.com
25. http://en.wikibooks.org/wiki/Subject:Social sciences
26. http://betanews.com/2013/04/30/miranda-ng-is-a-multi-protocol-im-client-with-style/